Fanny and the Servant Problem

by

Jerome K. Jerome

British Library Cataloguing-in-Publication Data
A catalogue record for this book is available from the
British Library

Jerome K. Jerome

Jerome Klapka Jerome was born in Walsall, England in 1859. Both his parents died while he was in his early teens, and he was forced to quit school to support himself. Jerome worked for a number of years collecting coal along railway tracks, before trying his hand at acting, journalism, teaching and soliciting. At long last, in 1885, he had some success with *On the Stage – and Off,* a comic memoir of his experiences with an acting troupe. Jerome produced a number of essays over the following years, and married in 1888, spending the honeymoon in "a little boat" on the Thames.

In 1889, Jerome published his most successful and best-remembered work, *Three Men in a Boat.* Featuring himself and two of his friends encountering humorous situations while floating down the Thames in a small boat, the book was an instant success, and has never been out of print. In fact, its popularity was such that the number of registered Thames boats went up fifty percent in the year following its publication. With the financial security provided by *Three Men in a Boat,* Jerome was able to dedicate himself fully to writing, producing eleven more novels and a number of anthologies of short fiction.

In 1926, Jerome published his autobiography, *My Life and Times.* He died a year later, aged 68.

THE CHARACTERS

Fanny
Her Husband, Vernon Wetherell, Lord Bantock
Her Butler, Martin Bennet
Her Housekeeper, Susannah Bennet
Her Maid, Jane Bennet
Her Second Footman, Ernest Bennet
Her Still-room Maid, Honoria Bennet
Her Aunts by marriage, the Misses Wetherell
Her Local Medical Man, Dr. Freemantle
Her quondam Companions, "Our Empire":
 England
 Scotland
 Ireland
 Wales
 Canada
 Australia
 New Zealand
 Africa
 India
 Newfoundland
 Malay Archipelago
 Straits Settlements
Her former Business Manager, George P. Newte

ACT I

SCENE

The Lady Bantock's boudoir, Bantock Hall, Rutlandshire, a spacious room handsomely furnished (chiefly in the style of Louis the Fourteenth) and lighted by three high windows, facing the south-west. A door between the fireplace and the windows leads to his lordship's apartments. A door the other side of the fireplace is the general entrance. The door opposite the windows leads through her ladyship's dressing-room into her ladyship's bedroom. Over the great fireplace hangs a full-length portrait of Constance, first Lady Bantock, by Hoppner.

The time is sunset of a day in early spring. The youthful Lord Bantock is expected home with his newly wedded wife this evening; and the two Misses Wetherell, his aunts, have been busy decorating the room with flowers, and are nearing the end of their labours. The two Misses Wetherell have grown so much alike it would be difficult for a stranger to tell one from the other; and to add to his confusion they have fallen into the habit of dressing much alike in a fashion of their own that went out long ago, while the hair of both is white, and even in their voices they have caught each other's tones.

THE ELDER MISS WETHERELL [she has paused from her work and is looking out of the windows]. Such a lovely sunset, dear.

THE YOUNGER MISS WETHERELL [she leaves her work and joins her sister. The two stand holding each other's hands, looking out]. Beautiful! [A silence. The sun is streaming full into the room.] You—you don't think, dear, that this room—[she looks round it]—may possibly be a little TOO sunny to quite suit her?

THE ELDER MISS WETHERELL [not at first understanding]. How, dear, TOO sun—[She grasps the meaning.] You mean—you think that perhaps she does that sort of thing?

THE YOUNGER MISS WETHERELL. Well, dear, one is always given to understand that they do, women—ladies of her profession.

THE ELDER MISS WETHERELL. It seems to me so wicked: painting God's work.

THE YOUNGER MISS WETHERELL. We mustn't judge hardly, dear. Besides, dear, we don't know yet that she does.

THE ELDER MISS WETHERELL. Perhaps she's young, and hasn't commenced it. I fancy it's only the older ones that do it.

THE YOUNGER MISS WETHERELL. He didn't mention her age, I remember.

THE ELDER MISS WETHERELL. No, dear, but I feel she's young.

THE YOUNGER MISS WETHERELL. I do hope she is. We may be able to mould her.

THE ELDER MISS WETHERELL. We must be very sympathetic. One can accomplish so much with sympathy.

THE YOUNGER MISS WETHERELL. We must get to understand her. [A sudden thought.] Perhaps, dear, we may get to like her.

THE ELDER MISS WETHERELL [doubtful]. We might TRY, dear.

THE YOUNGER MISS WETHERELL. For Vernon's sake. The poor boy seems so much in love with her. We must -

[Bennet has entered. He is the butler.]

BENNET. Doctor Freemantle. I have shown him into the library.

THE YOUNGER MISS WETHERELL. Thank you, Bennet. Will you please tell him that we shall be down in a few minutes? I must just finish these flowers. [She returns to the table.]

THE ELDER MISS WETHERELL. Why not ask him to come up here? We could consult him—about the room. He always knows everything.

THE YOUNGER MISS WETHERELL. A good idea. Please ask him, Bennet, if he would mind coming up to us here. [Bennet, who has been piling up fresh logs upon the fire, turns to go.] Oh, Bennet! You will remind Charles to put a footwarmer in the carriage!

BENNET. I will see to it myself. [He goes out.]

THE YOUNGER MISS WETHERELL. Thank you, Bennet. [To her sister] One's feet are always so cold after a railway journey.

THE ELDER MISS WETHERELL. I've been told that, nowadays, they heat the carriages.

THE YOUNGER MISS WETHERELL. Ah, it is an age of luxury! I wish I knew which were her favourite flowers. It is so nice to be greeted by one's favourite flowers.

THE ELDER MISS WETHERELL. I feel sure she loves lilies.

THE YOUNGER MISS WETHERELL. And they are so appropriate to a bride. So -

[Announced by Bennet, Dr. Freemantle bustles in. He is a dapper little man, clean-shaven, with quick brisk ways.]

DR. FREEMANTLE [he shakes hands]. Well, and how are we this afternoon? [He feels the pulse of the Younger Miss Wetherell] Steadier. Much steadier! [of the Elder Miss Wetherell.] Nervous tension greatly relieved.

THE YOUNGER MISS WETHERELL. She has been sleeping much better.

DR. FREEMANTLE [he pats the hand of the Elder Miss Wetherell]. Excellent! Excellent!

THE ELDER MISS WETHERELL. She ate a good breakfast this morning.

DR. FREEMANTLE [he pats the hand of the Younger Miss Wetherell]. Couldn't have a better sign. [He smiles from one to the other.] Brain disturbance, caused by futile opposition to the inevitable, evidently abating. One page Marcus Aurelius every morning before breakfast. "Adapt thyself," says Marcus Aurelius, "to the things with which thy lot has been cast. Whatever happens—"

THE YOUNGER MISS WETHERELL. You see, doctor, it was all so sudden.

DR. FREEMANTLE. The unexpected! It has a way of taking us by surprise—bowling us over—completely. Till we pull ourselves together. Make the best of what can't be helped—like brave, sweet gentlewomen. [He presses their hands. They are both wiping away a tear.] When do you expect them?

THE ELDER MISS WETHERELL. To-night, by the half-past eight train. We had a telegram this morning from Dover.

DR. FREEMANTLE. Um! and this is to be her room? [He takes it in.] The noble and renowned Constance, friend and confidant of the elder Pitt, maker of history, first Lady Bantock—by Hoppner—always there to keep an eye on her, remind her of the family traditions. Brilliant idea, brilliant! [They are both smiling with pleasure.]

THE ELDER MISS WETHERELL. And you don't think—it is what we wanted to ask you—that there is any fear of her finding it a little trying- -the light? You see, this is an exceptionally sunny room.

THE YOUNGER MISS WETHERELL. And these actresses—if all one hears is true -

[The dying sun is throwing his last beams across the room.]

DR. FREEMANTLE. Which, thank God, it isn't. [He seats himself in a large easy-chair. The two ladies sit side by side on a settee.] I'll tell you just exactly what you've got to expect. A lady—a few years older than the boy himself, but still young. Exquisite figure; dressed— perhaps a trifle too regardless of expense. Hair—maybe just a shade TOO golden. All that can be altered. Features— piquant, with expressive eyes, the use of which she probably understands, and an almost permanent smile, displaying an admirably preserved and remarkably even set of teeth. But, above all, clever. That's our sheet-anchor. The woman's clever. She will know how to adapt herself to her new position.

THE YOUNGER MISS WETHERELL [turning to her sister]. Yes, she must be clever to have obtained the position that she has. [To the Doctor] Vernon says that she was quite the chief attraction all this winter, in Paris.

THE ELDER MISS WETHERELL. And the French public is so critical.

DR. FREEMANTLE [drily]. Um! I was thinking rather of her cleverness in "landing" poor Vernon. The lad's not a fool.

THE ELDER MISS WETHERELL. We must do her justice. I think she was really in love with him.

DR. FREEMANTLE [still more drily]. Very possibly. Most cafe- chantant singers, I take it, would be—with an English lord. [He laughs.]

THE ELDER MISS WETHERELL. You see, she didn't know he was a lord.

DR. FREEMANTLE. Didn't know—?

THE YOUNGER MISS WETHERELL. No. She married him, thinking him to be a plain Mr. Wetherell, an artist.

DR. FREEMANTLE. Where d'ye get all that from?

THE ELDER MISS WETHERELL. From Vernon himself. You've got his last letter, dear. [She has opened her chatelaine bag.] Oh, no, I've got it myself.

THE YOUNGER MISS WETHERELL. He's not going to break it to her till they reach here this evening.

THE ELDER MISS WETHERELL [she reads]. Yes. "I shall not break it to her before we reach home. We were married quietly at the Hotel de Ville, and she has no idea I am anything else than plain Vernon James Wetherell, a fellow-countryman of her own, and a fellow-artist. The dear creature has never even inquired whether I am rich or poor." I like her for that.

DR. FREEMANTLE. You mean to tell me—[He jumps up. With his hands in his jacket pockets, he walks to and fro.] I suppose it's possible.

THE ELDER MISS WETHERELL. You see, she isn't the ordinary class of music-hall singer.

DR. FREEMANTLE. I should say not.

THE ELDER MISS WETHERELL. She comes of quite a good family.

THE YOUNGER MISS WETHERELL. Her uncle was a bishop.

DR. FREEMANTLE. Bishop? Of where?

THE ELDER MISS WETHERELL [with the letter]. He says he can't spell it. It's somewhere in New Zealand.

DR. FREEMANTLE. Do they have bishops over there?

THE YOUNGER MISS WETHERELL. Well, evidently.

THE ELDER MISS WETHERELL. Then her cousin is a judge.

DR. FREEMANTLE. In New Zealand?

THE ELDER MISS WETHERELL [again referring to the letter]. No—in Ohio.

DR. FREEMANTLE. Seems to have been a somewhat scattered family.

THE YOUNGER MISS WETHERELL. People go about so much nowadays.

[Mrs. Bennet has entered. She is the housekeeper.]

MRS. BENNET [she is about to speak to the Misses Wetherell; sees the Doctor]. Good afternoon, doctor.

DR. FREEMANTLE. Afternoon, Mrs. Bennet.

MRS. BENNET [she turns to the Misses Wetherell, her watch in her hand]. I was thinking of having the fire lighted in her ladyship's bedroom. It is half past six.

THE ELDER MISS WETHERELL. You are always so thoughtful. She may be tired.

MRS. BENNET. If so, everything will be quite ready. [She goes out, closing door.]

DR. FREEMANTLE. What do they think about it all—the Bennets? You have told them?

THE YOUNGER MISS WETHERELL. We thought it better. You see, one hardly regards them as servants. They have been in the family so long. Three generations of them.

THE ELDER MISS WETHERELL. Really, since our poor dear brother's death, Bennet has been more like the head of the house than the butler.

THE YOUNGER MISS WETHERELL. Of course, he doesn't say much.

THE ELDER MISS WETHERELL. It is her having been on the stage that they feel so.

THE YOUNGER MISS WETHERELL. You see, they have always been a religious family.

THE ELDER MISS WETHERELL. Do you know, I really think they feel it more than we do. I found Peggy crying about it yesterday, in the scullery.

DR. FREEMANTLE [he has been listening with a touch of amusement.] Peggy Bennet?

THE YOUNGER MISS WETHERELL. Yes. CHARLES Bennet's daughter.

DR. FREEMANTLE. Happen to have a servant about the place who isn't a Bennet?

THE YOUNGER MISS WETHERELL. No, no, I don't really think we have. Oh, yes—that new girl Mrs. Bennet engaged last week for the dairy. What is her name?

THE ELDER MISS WETHERELL. Arnold.

THE YOUNGER MISS WETHERELL. Ah, yes, Arnold.

DR. FREEMANTLE. Ah!

THE ELDER MISS WETHERELL. I think she's a cousin, dear.

THE YOUNGER MISS WETHERELL. Only a second cousin.

DR. FREEMANTLE. Um! Well I should tell the whole family to buck up. Seems to me, from what you tell me, that their master is bringing them home a treasure. [He shakes hands briskly with the ladies.] May look in again to-morrow. Don't forget—one page Marcus Aurelius before breakfast—in case of need. [He goes out.]

[The sun has sunk. The light is twilight.]

THE ELDER MISS WETHERELL. He always cheers one up.

THE YOUNGER MISS WETHERELL. He's so alive. [Mrs. Bennet comes in from the dressing-room. She leaves the door ajar. The sound of a hammer is heard. It ceases almost immediately.] Oh, Mrs. Bennet, we were going to ask you—who is to be her ladyship's maid? Have you decided yet?

MRS. BENNET. I have come to the conclusion— looking at the thing from every point of view—that Jane would be the best selection.

THE YOUNGER MISS WETHERELL. Jane!

THE ELDER MISS WETHERELL. But does she understand the duties?

MRS. BENNET. A lady's maid, being so much alone with her mistress, is bound to have a certain amount of influence. And Jane has exceptionally high principles.

THE YOUNGER MISS WETHERELL. That is true, dear.

MRS. BENNET. As regards the duties, she is very quick at learning anything new. Of course, at first -

[The sound of hammering again comes from the bedroom.]

THE YOUNGER MISS WETHERELL. Who is that hammering in her ladyship's bedroom?

MRS. BENNET. It is Bennet, Miss Edith. We thought it might be helpful: a few texts, hung where they would always catch her ladyship's eye. [She notices the look of doubt.] Nothing offensive. Mere general exhortations such as could be read by any lady. [The Misses Wetherell look at one another, but do not speak.] I take it, dinner will be at half past seven, as usual?

THE ELDER MISS WETHERELL. Yes, Mrs. Bennet, thank you. They will not be here till about nine. They will probably prefer a little supper to themselves.

[Mrs. Bennet goes out—on her way to the kitchen. The Misses Wetherell look at one another again. The hammering recommences.]

THE YOUNGER MISS WETHERELL [she hesitates a moment, then goes to the open door and calls]. Bennet—Bennet! [She returns and waits. Bennet comes in.] Oh, Bennet, your wife tells us you are putting up a few texts in her ladyship's bedroom.

BENNET. It seemed to me that a silent voice, speaking to her, as it were, from the wall -

THE YOUNGER MISS WETHERELL. It is so good of you—only, you—you will be careful there is nothing she could regard as a PERSONAL allusion.

BENNET. Many of the most popular I was compelled to reject, purely for that reason.

THE ELDER MISS WETHERELL. We felt sure we could trust to your discretion.

THE YOUNGER MISS WETHERELL. You see, coming, as she does, from a good family -

BENNET. It is that—I speak merely for myself—that gives me hope of reclaiming her.

[A silence. The two ladies, feeling a little helpless, again look at one another.]

THE ELDER MISS WETHERELL. We must be very sympathetic.

THE YOUNGER MISS WETHERELL. And patient, Bennet.

BENNET. It is what I am preparing myself to be. Of course, if you think them inadvisable, I can take them down again.

THE YOUNGER MISS WETHERELL. No, Bennet, oh no! I should leave them up. Very thoughtful of you, indeed.

BENNET. It seemed to me one ought to leave no stone unturned. [He returns to his labours in the bedroom.]

THE YOUNGER MISS WETHERELL [after a pause]. I do hope she'll LIKE the Bennets.

THE ELDER MISS WETHERELL. I think she will— after a time, when she is used to them.

THE YOUNGER MISS WETHERELL. I am so anxious it should turn out well.

THE ELDER MISS WETHERELL. I feel sure she's a good woman. Vernon would never have fallen in love with her if she hadn't been good. [They take each other's hand, and sit side by side, as before, upon the settee. The twilight has faded: only the faint firelight remains, surrounded by shadows.] Do you remember, when he was a little mite, how he loved to play with your hair? [The younger Miss Wetherell laughs.] I always envied you your hair.

THE YOUNGER MISS WETHERELL. He was so fond of us both. Do you remember when he was recovering from the measles, his crying for us to bath him instead of Mrs. Bennet? I have always reproached myself that we refused.

THE ELDER MISS WETHERELL. He was such a big boy for his age.

THE YOUNGER MISS WETHERELL. I think we might have stretched a point in a case of illness.

[The room has grown very dark. The door has been softly opened; Vernon and Fanny have entered noiselessly. Fanny remains near the door hidden by a screen, Vernon has crept forward. At this point the two ladies become aware that somebody is in the room. They are alarmed.]

THE ELDER MISS WETHERELL. Who's there?

VERNON. It's all right, aunt. It's only I.

[The two ladies have risen. They run forward, both take him in their arms.]

THE YOUNGER MISS WETHERELL. Vernon!

THE ELDER MISS WETHERELL. My dear boy!

THE YOUNGER MISS WETHERELL. But we didn't expect you -

THE ELDER MISS WETHERELL. And your wife, dear?

VERNON. She's here!

THE ELDER MISS WETHERELL. Here?

[Fanny, from behind the screen, laughs.]

VERNON. We'll have some light. [He whispers to them.] Not a word— haven't told her yet. [Feeling his way to the wall, he turns on the electric light.]

[Fanny is revealed, having slipped out from behind the screen. There is a pause. Vernon, standing near the fire, watches admiringly.]

FANNY. Hope you are going to like me.

THE YOUNGER MISS WETHERELL. My dear, I am sure we shall.

THE ELDER MISS WETHERELL. It is so easy to love the young and pretty. [They have drawn close to her. They seem to hesitate.]

FANNY [laughs]. It doesn't come off, does it, Vernon, dear? [Vernon laughs. The two ladies, laughing, kiss her.] I'm so glad you think I'm pretty. As a matter of fact, I'm not. There's a certain charm about me, I admit. It deceives people.

THE YOUNGER MISS WETHERELL. We were afraid—you know, dear, boys— [she looks at Vernon and smiles] sometimes fall in love with women much older than themselves—especially women—[She grows confused. She takes the girl's hand.] We are so relieved that you—that you are yourself, dear,

FANNY. You were quite right, dear. They are sweet. Which is which?

VERNON [laughs]. Upon my word, I never can tell.

THE YOUNGER MISS WETHERELL. Vernon! And you know I was always your favourite!

THE ELDER MISS WETHERELL. Dear!

VERNON. Then this is Aunt Alice.

THE YOUNGER MISS WETHERELL. No dear, Edith.

[Vernon throws up his hands in despair. They all laugh.]

FANNY. I think I shall dress you differently; put you in blue and you in pink. [She laughs.] Is this the drawing-room?

VERNON. Your room, dear.

FANNY. I like a room where one can stretch one's legs. [She walks across it.] A little too much desk [referring to a massive brass- bound desk, facing the three windows].

THE ELDER MISS WETHERELL. It belonged to the elder Pitt.

FANNY. Um! Suppose we must find a corner for it somewhere. That's a good picture.

THE YOUNGER MISS WETHERELL. It is by Hoppner.

FANNY. One of your artist friends?

VERNON. Well—you see, dear, that's a portrait of my great- grandmother, painted from life.

FANNY [she whistles]. I am awfully ignorant on some topics. One good thing, I always was a quick study. Not a bad-looking woman.

THE ELDER MISS WETHERELL. We are very proud of her. She was the first -

VERNON [hastily]. We will have her history some other time.

THE YOUNGER MISS WETHERELL [who understands, signs to her sister]. Of course. She's tired. We are forgetting everything. You will have some tea, won't you, dear?

FANNY. No, thanks. We had tea in the train. [With the more or less helpful assistance of Vernon she divests herself of her outdoor garments.]

THE ELDER MISS WETHERELL [she holds up her hands in astonishment]. Tea in the train!

THE YOUNGER MISS WETHERELL. We were not expecting you so soon. You said in your telegram -

VERNON. Oh, it was raining in London. We thought we would come straight on—leave our shopping for another day.

FANNY. I believe you were glad it was raining. Saved you such a lot of money. Old Stingy!

THE ELDER MISS WETHERELL. Then did you walk from the station, dear?

FANNY. Didn't it seem a long way? [She laughs up into his face.] He was so bored. [Vernon laughs.]

THE YOUNGER MISS WETHERELL. I had better tell—[She is going towards the bell.]

VERNON [he stops her]. Oh, let them alone. Plenty of time for all that fuss. [He puts them both gently side by side on the settee.] Sit down and talk. Haven't I been clever? [He puts his arm round Fanny, laughing.] You thought I had made an ass of myself, didn't you? Did you get all my letters?

THE YOUNGER MISS WETHERELL. I think so, dear.

FANNY [she is sitting in an easy-chair. Vernon seats himself on the arm]. Do you know I've never had a love-letter from you?

VERNON. You gave me no time. She met me a month ago, and married me last week.

FANNY. It was quick work. He came—he saw—I conquered! [Laughs.]

THE ELDER MISS WETHERELL. They say that love at first sight is often the most lasting.

VERNON [he puts his arm around her]. You are sure you will never regret having given up the stage? The excitement, the -

FANNY. The excitement! Do you know what an actress's life always seemed to me like? Dancing on a tight-rope with everybody throwing stones at you. One soon gets tired of that sort of excitement. Oh, I was never in love with the stage. Had to do something for a living.

THE YOUNGER MISS WETHERELL. It must be a hard life for a woman.

THE ELDER MISS WETHERELL. Especially for anyone not brought up to it.

FANNY. You see, I had a good voice and what I suppose you might call a natural talent for acting. It seemed the easiest thing.

THE YOUNGER MISS WETHERELL. I suppose your family were very much opposed to it? [Vernon rises. He stands with his back to the fire.]

FANNY. My family? Hadn't any!

THE ELDER MISS WETHERELL. No family?

[Bennet enters. Vernon and Fanny left the door open. He halts, framed by the doorway.]

FANNY. No. You see, I was an only child. My father and mother both died before I was fourteen.

THE YOUNGER MISS WETHERELL. But your uncle?

FANNY. Oh, him! It was to get away from him and all that crew that I went on the stage.

THE ELDER MISS WETHERELL. It is so sad when relations don't get on together.

FANNY. Sadder still when they think they've got a right to trample on you, just because you happen to be an orphan and—I don't want to talk about my relations. I want to forget them. I stood them for nearly six months. I don't want to be reminded of them. I want to forget that they ever existed. I want to forget -

[Bennet has come down very quietly. Fanny, from where he stands, is the only one who sees him. He stands looking at her, his features, as ever, immovable. At sight of him her eyes and mouth open wider and wider. The words die away from her tongue. Vernon has turned away to put a log on the fire, and so has not seen her expression— only hears her sudden silence. He looks up and sees Bennet.]

VERNON. Ah, Bennet! [He advances, holding out his hand.] You quite well?

BENNET [shaking hands with him]. Quite well.

VERNON. Good! And all the family?

BENNET. Nothing to complain of. Charles has had a touch of influenza.

VERNON. Ah, sorry to hear that.

BENNET. And your lordship?

VERNON. Fit as a fiddle—your new mistress.

Fanny has risen. Bennet turns to her. For a moment his back is towards the other three. Fanny alone sees his face.

BENNET. We shall endeavour to do our duty to her ladyship. [He turns to Vernon.] I had arranged for a more fitting reception -

VERNON. To tell the honest truth, Bennet, the very thing we were afraid of—why we walked from the station, and slipped in by the side door. [Laughing.] Has the luggage come?

BENNET. It has just arrived. It was about that I came to ask. I could not understand -

[The Misses Wetherell have also risen. Fanny's speechless amazement is attributed by them and Vernon to natural astonishment at discovery of his rank.]

THE YOUNGER MISS WETHERELL. You will be wanting a quiet talk together. We shall see you at dinner.

VERNON. What time is dinner?

THE YOUNGER MISS WETHERELL. Half past seven. [To Fanny] But don't you hurry, dear. I will tell cook to delay it a little. [She kisses her.]

THE ELDER MISS WETHERELL. You will want some time to arrange that pretty hair of yours. [She also kisses the passive, speechless Fanny. They go out hand in hand.]

BENNET. I will see, while I am here, that your lordship's room is in order.

VERNON. Why, where's Robert, then?

BENNET. He has gone into town to do some shopping. We did not expect your lordship much before nine. There may be one or two things to see to. [He goes into his lordship's apartments, closing the door behind him.]

FANNY. Vernon, where am I?

VERNON. At home, dear.

FANNY. Yes, but where?

VERNON. At Bantock Hall, Rutlandshire. [Fanny sits down on the settee—drops down rather.] You're not angry with me? You know how the world always talks in these cases. I wanted to be able to prove to them all that you married me for myself. Not because I was Lord Bantock. Can you forgive me?

FANNY [she still seems in a dream]. Yes—of course. You didn't—you wouldn't—[She suddenly springs up.] Vernon, you do love me? [She flings her arms round his neck.]

VERNON. Dear!

FANNY. You will never be ashamed of me?

VERNON. Dearest!

FANNY. I was only a music-hall singer. There's no getting over it, you know.

VERNON. I should have loved you had you been a beggar-maid.

FANNY [she still clings to him]. With an uncle a costermonger, and an aunt who sold matches. It wouldn't have made any difference to you, would it? You didn't marry me for my family, did you? You didn't, did you?

VERNON. Darling! I married you because you are the most fascinating, the most lovable, the most wonderful little woman in the world. [Fanny gives a sob.] As for your family—I've got a confession to make to you, dear. I made inquiries about your family before I proposed to you. Not for my own sake—because I knew I'd have to answer a lot of stupid questions. It seemed to me quite a good family.

FANNY. It is! Oh, it is! There never was such a respectable family. That's why I never could get on with them.

VERNON [laughing]. Well, you haven't got to—any more. We needn't even let them know -

[Bennet returns.]

BENNET. Robert I find has returned. It is ten minutes to seven.

VERNON. Thanks. Well, I shall be glad of a bath. [He turns to Fanny.] Bennet will send your maid to you. [He whispers to her.] You'll soon get used to it all. As for the confounded family—we will forget all about them. [Fanny answers with another little stifled sob. Bennet is drawing the curtains, his back to the room. Vernon, seeing that Bennet is occupied, kisses the unresponsive Fanny and goes out.]

[At the sound of the closing of the door, Fanny looks up. She goes to the door through which Vernon has just passed, listens a moment, then returns. Bennet calmly finishes the drawing of the curtains. Then he, too, crosses slowly till he and Fanny are facing one another across the centre of the room.]

FANNY. Well, what are you going to do?

BENNET. My duty!

FANNY. What's that? Something unpleasant, I know. I can bet my bottom dollar.

BENNET. That, my girl, will depend upon you.

FANNY. How upon me?

BENNET. Whether you prove an easy or a difficult subject. To fit you for your position, a certain amount of training will, I fancy, be necessary.

FANNY. Training! I'm to be—[She draws herself up.] Are you aware who I am?

BENNET. Oh yes. AND who you were. His lordship, I take it, would hardly relish the discovery that he had married his butler's niece. He might consider the situation awkward.

FANNY. And who's going to train me?

BENNET. I am. With the assistance of your aunt and such other members of your family as I consider can be trusted.

FANNY [for a moment she is speechless, then she bursts out]. That ends it! I shall tell him! I shall tell him this very moment. [She sweeps towards the door.]

BENNET. At this moment you will most likely find his lordship in his bath.

FANNY. I don't care! Do you think—do you think for a moment that I'm going to allow myself—I, Lady Bantock, to be—[Her hand upon the door.] I shall tell him, and you'll only have yourself to blame. He loves me. He loves me for myself. I shall tell him the whole truth, and ask him to give you all the sack.

BENNET. You're not forgetting that you've already told him ONCE who you were?

[It stops her. What she really did was to leave the marriage arrangements in the hands of her business manager, George P. Newte. As agent for a music-hall star, he is ideal, but it is possible that in answering Lord Bantock's inquiries concerning Fanny's antecedents he may not have kept strictly to the truth.]

FANNY. I never did. I've never told him anything about my family.

BENNET. Curious. I was given to understand it was rather a classy affair.

FANNY. I can't help what other people may have done. Because some silly idiot of a man may possibly—[She will try a new tack. She leaves the door and comes to him.] Uncle, dear, wouldn't it be simpler for you all to go away? He's awfully fond of me. He'll do anything I ask him. I could merely say that I didn't like you and get him to pension you off. You and aunt could have a little roadside inn somewhere—with ivy.

BENNET. Seeing that together with the stables and the garden there are twenty-three of us -

FANNY. No, of course, he couldn't pension you all. You couldn't expect -

BENNET. I think his lordship might prefer to leave things as they are. Good servants nowadays are not so easily replaced. And neither your aunt nor I are at an age when change appeals to one.

FANNY. You see, it's almost bound to creep out sooner or later, and then -

BENNET. We will make it as late as possible [He crosses and rings the bell], giving you time to prove to his lordship that you are not incapable of learning.

FANNY [she drops back on the settee. She is half-crying.] Some people would be pleased that their niece had married well.

BENNET. I am old-fashioned enough to think also of my duty to those I serve. If his lordship has done me the honour to marry my niece, the least I can is to see to it that she brings no discredit to his name. [Mrs. Bennet, followed by Jane Bennet, a severe-looking woman of middle age, has entered upon the words "the least I can do." Bennet stays them a moment with his hand while he finishes. Then he turns to his wife.] You will be interested to find, Susannah, that the new Lady Bantock is not a stranger.

MRS. BENNET. Not a stranger! [She has reached a position from where she sees the girl.] Fanny! You wicked girl! Where have you been all these years?

BENNET [interposing]. There will be other opportunities for the discussion of family differences. Just now, her ladyship is waiting to dress for dinner.

MRS. BENNET [sneering]. Her ladyship!

JANE [also sneering]. I think she might have forewarned us of the honour in store for us.

MRS. BENNET. Yes, why didn't she write?

FANNY. Because I didn't know. Do you think—[she rises]—that if I had I would ever have married him—to be brought back here and put in this ridiculous position? Do you think that I am so fond of you all that I couldn't keep away from you, at any price?

MRS. BENNET. But you must have known that Lord Bantock -

FANNY. I didn't know he was Lord Bantock. I only knew him as Mr. Wetherell, an artist. He wanted to feel sure that I was marrying him for himself alone. He never told me—[Ernest Bennet, a very young footman, has entered in answer to Bennet's ring of a minute ago. He has come forward step by step, staring all the while open-mouthed at Fanny. Turning, she sees him beside her.] Hulloa, Ernie. How are the rabbits? [She kisses him.]

BENNET. Don't stand there gaping. I rang for some wood. Tell your brother dinner will be at a quarter to eight.

[Ernest, never speaking, still staring at Fanny, gets clumsily out again.]

FANNY. Well, I suppose I'd better see about dressing? Do I dine with his lordship or in the servants' hall?

MRS. BENNET [turns to her husband]. You see! Still the old impertinence.

FANNY. Only wanted to know. My only desire is to give satisfaction.

BENNET [he moves towards the door]. You will do it by treating the matter more seriously. At dinner, by keeping your eye upon me, you will be able to tell whether you are behaving yourself or not.

MRS. BENNET. And mind you are punctual. I have appointed Jane to be your maid.

FANNY. Jane!

MRS. BENNET [in arms]. Have you any objections?

FANNY. No, oh no, so long as you're all satisfied.

MRS. BENNET. Remember, you are no longer on the music-hall   stage.
In dressing for Bantock Hall you will do well to follow her advice.

[Bennet, who has been waiting with the door in his hand, goes out; Mrs. Bennet follows.]

JANE [in the tones of a patient executioner]. Are you ready?

FANNY. Quite ready, dear. Of course—I don't know what you will think of them—but I've only brought modern costumes with me.

JANE [not a lady who understands satire]. We must do the best we can. [She marches out—into the dressing-room.]

[Fanny, after following a few steps, stops and thinks. Ernest has entered with the wood. He is piling it in the basket by the fire. His entrance decides her. She glances through the open door of the dressing-room, then flies across to the desk, seats herself, and begins feverishly to write a telegram.]

FANNY. Ernie! [He comes across to her.] Have you still got your bicycle?

ERNEST. Yes.

FANNY. Could you get this telegram off for me before eight o'clock? I don't want it sent from the village; I want you to take it YOURSELF—into the town. There's a sovereign for you if you do it all right.

ERNEST. I'll do it. Can only get into a row.

FANNY. Pretty used to them, ain't you? [She has risen. She gives him the telegram. She has stamped it.] Can you read it?

ERNEST. "George P. Newte."

FANNY. Hush!

[They both glance at the open door.]

ERNEST [he continues in a lower voice]. "72A, Waterloo Bridge Road, London. Must see you at once. Am at the new shop." [He looks up.]

FANNY. That's all right.

ERNEST. "Come down. Q.T. Fanny."

FANNY [nods]. Get off quietly. I'll see you again -

THE VOICE OF JANE [from the dressing-room]. Are you going to keep me waiting all night?

[They start. Ernest hastily thrusts the telegram into his breast- pocket.]

FANNY. Coming, dear, coming. [To Ernest] Not a word to anyone! [She hurries him out and closes door behind him.] Merely been putting the room a bit tidy. [She is flying round collecting her outdoor garments.] Thought it would please you. So sorry if I've kept you waiting. [Jane has appeared at door.] After you, dear.

[Jane goes out again. Fanny, with her pile of luggage, follows.]

[CURTAIN]

ACT II

SCENE

The same.

Time.—The next morning.

[The door opens. Dr. Freemantle enters, shown in by Bennet, who follows him.]

DR. FREEMANTLE [talking as he enters]. Wonderful! Wonderful! I don't really think I ever remember so fine a spring.

BENNET [he is making up the fire]. I'm afraid we shall have to pay for it later on.

DR. FREEMANTLE. I expect so. Law of the universe, you know, Bennet- -law of the universe. Everything in this world has got to be paid for.

BENNET. Except trouble. [The doctor laughs.] The Times? [He hands it to him.]

DR. FREEMANTLE. Thanks. Thanks. [Seats himself.] Won't be long— his lordship, will he?

BENNET. I don't think so. I told him you would be here about eleven.

DR. FREEMANTLE. Um—what do you think of her?

BENNET. Of—of her ladyship?

DR. FREEMANTLE. What's she like?

BENNET. [They have sunk their voices.] Well, it might have been worse.

DR. FREEMANTLE. Ah! There's always that consolation, isn't there?

BENNET. I think her ladyship—with MANAGEMENT—may turn out very satisfactory.

DR. FREEMANTLE. You like her?

BENNET. At present, I must say for her, she appears willing to be taught.

DR. FREEMANTLE. And you think it will last?

BENNET. I think her ladyship appreciates the peculiarity of her position. I will tell the Miss Wetherells you are here.

DR. FREEMANTLE. Ah, thanks!

BENNET. I fancy her ladyship will not herself be visible much before lunch time. I understand she woke this morning with a headache. [He goes out.]

[The Doctor reads a moment. Then the door of the dressing-room opens, and Fanny enters. Her dress is a wonderful contrast to her costume of last evening. It might be that of a poor and demure nursery governess. Her hair is dressed in keeping. She hardly seems the same woman.]

FANNY [seeing the Doctor, she pauses]. Oh!

DR. FREEMANTLE [rises]. I beg pardon, have I the pleasure of seeing Lady Bantock?

FANNY. Yes.

DR. FREEMANTLE. Delighted. May I introduce myself—Dr. Freemantle? I helped your husband into the world.

FANNY. Yes. I've heard of you. You don't mind my closing this door, do you? [Her very voice and manner are changed.]

DR. FREEMANTLE [a little puzzled]. Not at all.

FANNY [she closes the door and returns]. Won't—won't you be seated?

DR. FREEMANTLE. Thanks. [They both sit.] How's the headache?

FANNY. Oh, it's better.

DR. FREEMANTLE. Ah! [A silence.] Forgive me—I'm an old friend of the family. You're not a bit what I expected.

FANNY. But you like it? I mean you think this—[with a gesture]—is all right?

DR. FREEMANTLE. My dear young lady, it's charming. You couldn't be anything else.

FANNY. Thank you.

DR. FREEMANTLE. I merely meant that—well, I was not expecting anything so delightfully demure.

FANNY. That's the idea—"seemly." The Lady Bantocks have always been "seemly"? [She puts it as a question.]

DR. FREEMANTLE [more and more puzzled]. Yes— oh, yes. They have always been—[His eye catches that of Constance, first Lady Bantock, looking down at him from above the chimney-piece. His tone changes.] Well, yes, in their way, you know.

FANNY. You see, I'm in the difficult position of following her LATE ladyship. SHE appears to have been exceptionally "seemly." This is her frock. I mean it WAS her frock.

DR. FREEMANTLE. God bless my soul! You are not dressing yourself up in her late ladyship's clothes? The dear good woman has been dead and buried these twenty years.

FANNY [she looks at her dress]. Yes, it struck me as being about that period.

DR. FREEMANTLE [he goes across to her]. What's the trouble? Too much Bennet?

FANNY [she looks up. There is a suspicion of a smile]. One might say—sufficient?

DR. FREEMANTLE [laughs]. Excellent servants. If they'd only remember it. [He glances round—sinks his voice.] Take my advice. Put your foot down—before it's too late.

FANNY. Sit down, please. [She makes room for him on the   settee.] Because I'm going to be confidential. You don't mind, do you?

DR. FREEMANTLE [seating himself]. My dear, I take it as the greatest compliment I have had paid to me for years.

FANNY. You put everything so nicely. I'm two persons. I'm an angel—perhaps that is too strong a word?

DR. FREEMANTLE [doubtfully]. Well -

FANNY. We'll say saint. Or else I'm—the other thing.

DR. FREEMANTLE. Do you know, I think you could be.

FANNY. It's not a question about which there is any doubt.

DR. FREEMANTLE. Of course, in this case, a LITTLE bit of the devil -

FANNY [she shakes her head]. There's such a lot of mine. It has always hampered me, never being able to hit the happy medium.

DR. FREEMANTLE. It IS awkward.

FANNY. I thought I would go on being an angel -

DR. FREEMANTLE. Saint.

FANNY. Saint—till—well, till it became physically impossible to be a saint any longer.

DR. FREEMANTLE. And then?

FANNY [she rises, turns to him with a gesture of half-comic, half- tragic despair]. Well, then I can't help it, can I?

DR. FREEMANTLE. I think you're making a mistake. An explosion will undoubtedly have to take place. That being so, the sooner it takes place the better. [He rises.] What are you afraid of?

FANNY [she changes her tone—the talk becomes serious]. You've known Vernon all his life?

DR. FREEMANTLE. No one better.

FANNY. Tell me. I've known him only as a lover. What sort of a man is he?

[A pause. They are looking straight into each other's eyes.]

DR. FREEMANTLE. A man it pays to be perfectly frank with.

FANNY. It's a very old family, isn't it?

DR. FREEMANTLE. Old! Good Lord no! First Lord Bantock was only Vernon's great-grandfather. That is the woman that did it all. [He is looking at the Hoppner.]

FANNY. How do you mean?

DR. FREEMANTLE. Got them their title. Made the name of Bantock of importance in the history of the Georges. Clever woman.

FANNY [leaning over a chair, she is staring into the eyes of the first Lady Bantock]. I wonder what she would have done if she had ever got herself into a really first-class muddle?

DR. FREEMANTLE. One thing's certain. [Fanny turns to him.] She'd have got out of it.

FANNY [addresses the portrait]. I do wish you could talk.

[Vernon bursts into the room. He has been riding. He throws aside his hat and stick.]

VERNON. Hulloa! This is good of you. [He shakes hands with the Doctor.] How are you? [Without waiting for any reply, he goes to Fanny, kisses her.] Good morning, dear. How have you been getting on together, you two? Has she been talking to you?

DR. FREEMANTLE. Oh, yes.

VERNON. Doesn't she talk well? I say, what have you been doing to yourself?

FANNY. Jane thought this style—[with a gesture]— more appropriate to Lady Bantock.

VERNON. Um! Wonder if she's right? [To the Doctor] What do you think?

DR. FREEMANTLE. I think it a question solely for Lady Bantock.

VERNON. Of course it is. [To Fanny] You know, you mustn't let them dictate to you. Dear, good, faithful souls, all of them. But they must understand that you are mistress.

FANNY [she seizes eagerly at the chance]. You might mention it to them, dear. It would come so much better from you.

VERNON. No, you. They will take more notice of you.

FANNY. I'd so much rather you did it. [To Dr. Freemantle] Don't you think it would come better from him?

DR. FREEMANTLE [laughs]. I'm afraid you'll have to do it yourself.

VERNON. You see, dear, it might hurt them, coming from me. It would seem like ingratitude. Mrs. Bennet—Why, it wasn't till I began to ask questions that I grasped the fact that she WASN'T my real mother. As for old Bennet, ever since my father died—well, I hardly know how I could have got on without him. It was Charles Bennet that taught me to ride; I learned my letters sitting on Jane's lap.

FANNY. Yes. Perhaps I had better do it myself.

VERNON. I'm sure it will be more effective. Of course I shall support you.

FANNY. Thank you. Oh, by the by, dear, I shan't be able to go with you to-day.

VERNON. Why not?

FANNY. I've rather a headache.

VERNON. Oh, I'm so sorry. Oh, all right, we'll stop at home. I'm not so very keen about it.

FANNY. No, I want you to go, dear. Your aunts are looking forward to it. I shall get over it all the sooner with everybody out of the way.

VERNON. Well, if you really wish it.

[The Misses Wetherell steal in. They are dressed for driving. They exchange greetings with the Doctor.]

FANNY. You know you promised to obey. [Tickles his nose with a flower.]

VERNON [laughing—to the Doctor]. You see what it is to be married?

DR. FREEMANTLE [laughs]. Very trying.

VERNON [turning to his aunts]. Fanny isn't coming with us.

THE YOUNGER MISS WETHERELL [to Fanny]. Oh, my dear!

FANNY. It's only a headache. [She takes her aside.] I'm rather glad of it. I want an excuse for a little time to myself.

THE YOUNGER MISS WETHERELL. I understand, dear. It's all been so sudden. [She kisses her—then to the room] She'll be all the better alone. We three will go on. [She nods and signs to her sister.]

FANNY [kissing the Elder Miss Wetherell]. Don't you get betting.

THE ELDER MISS WETHERELL. Oh no, dear, we never do. It's just to see the dear horses. [She joins her sister. They whisper.]

VERNON [to the Doctor to whom he has been talking]. Can we give you a lift?

DR. FREEMANTLE. Well, you might as far as the Vicarage. Good-bye, Lady Bantock.

FANNY [shaking hands]. Good-bye, Doctor.

VERNON. Sure you won't be lonely?

FANNY [laughs]. Think I can't exist an hour without you? Mr. Conceited!

VERNON [laughs and kisses her]. Come along. [He takes the Doctor and his younger Aunt towards the door.]

THE ELDER MISS WETHERELL [who is following last]. I like you in that frock.

FANNY [laughs]. So glad. It's Ernest who attends to the fires, isn't it?

THE ELDER MISS WETHERELL. Yes, dear.

FANNY. I wish you'd send him up. [At door—calls after them] Hope you'll all enjoy yourselves!

VERNON [from the distance]. I shall put you on a fiver.

FANNY. Mind it wins. [She listens a moment—closes door, comes back to desk, and takes a Bradshaw.] Five-six-three—five-six-three. [Finds page.] St. Pancras, eight o'clock. Oh, Lord! Stamford, 10.45. Leave Stamford— [Ernest has entered.] Is that you, Ernest?

ERNEST. Yes.

FANNY. Shut the door. Sure it went off last night, that telegram?

ERNEST. Yes.

FANNY. If he doesn't catch that eight o'clock, he can't get here till nearly four. That will be awkward. [To Ernest] What time is it now?

ERNEST [looks at clock]. Twenty past eleven.

FANNY. If he does, he'll be here about twelve—I believe I'll go and meet him. Could I get out without being seen?

ERNEST. You'll have to pass the lodge.

FANNY. Who's at the lodge now?

ERNEST. Mother.

FANNY. Damn!

[Bennet has entered unnoticed and drawn near. At this point from behind, he boxes Ernest's ears.]

ERNEST. Here, steady!

BENNET. On the occasions when your cousin forgets her position, you will remember it and remind her of it. Get out! [Ernest, clumsily as ever, "gets out."] A sort of person has called who, according to his own account, "happened to be passing this way," and would like to see you.

FANNY [who has been trying to hide the Bradshaw—with affected surprise.] To see me!

BENNET [drily]. Yes. I thought you would be surprised. He claims to be an old friend of yours—Mr. George Newte.

FANNY [still keeping it up]. George Newte! Of course—ah, yes. Do you mind showing him up?

BENNET. I thought I would let you know he had arrived, in case you might be getting anxious about him. I propose giving him a glass of beer and sending him away again.

FANNY [flares up]. Look here, uncle, you and I have got to understand one another. I may put up with being bullied myself—if I can't see any help for it—but I'm not going to stand my friends being insulted. You show Mr. Newte up here.

[A silence.]

BENNET. I shall deem it my duty to inform his lordship of Mr. Newte's visit.

FANNY. There will be no need to. Mr. Newte, if his arrangements permit, will be staying to dinner.

BENNET. That, we shall see about. [He goes out.]

FANNY [following him to door]. And tell them I shall want the best bedroom got ready in case Mr. Newte is able to stay the night. I've done it. [She goes to piano, dashes into the "Merry Widow Waltz," or some other equally inappropriate but well-known melody, and then there enters Newte, shown in by Bennet. Newte is a cheerful person, attractively dressed in clothes suggestive of a successful bookmaker. He carries a white pot hat and tasselled cane. His gloves are large and bright. He is smoking an enormous cigar.]

BENNET. Mr. Newte.

FANNY [she springs up and greets him. They are evidently good friends] . Hulloa, George!

NEWTE. Hulloa, Fan—I beg your pardon, Lady Bantock. [Laughs.] Was just passing this way -

FANNY [cutting him short]. Yes. So nice of you to call.

NEWTE. I said to myself—[His eye catches Bennet; he stops.] Ah, thanks. [He gives Bennet his hat and stick, but Bennet does not seem satisfied. He has taken from the table a small china tray. This he is holding out to Newte, evidently for Newte to put something in it. But what? Newte is puzzled, he glances at Fanny. The idea strikes him that perhaps it is a tip Bennet is waiting for. It seems odd, but if it be the custom—he puts his hand to his trousers pocket.]

BENNET. The smoking-room is on the ground-floor.

NEWTE. Ah, my cigar. I beg your pardon. I couldn't understand. [He puts it on the tray—breaks into a laugh.]

BENNET. Thank you. Her ladyship is suffering from a headache. If I might suggest—a little less boisterousness. [He goes out.]

NEWTE [he watches him out]. I say, your Lord Chamberlain's a bit of a freezer!

FANNY. Yes. Wants hanging out in the sun. How did you manage to get here so early? [She sits.]

NEWTE. Well, your telegram rather upset me. I thought—correct etiquette for me to sit down here, do you think?

FANNY. Don't ask me. Got enough new tricks of my own to learn. [Laughs.] Should chance it, if I were you.

NEWTE. Such a long time since I was at Court. [He sits.] Yes, I was up at five o'clock this morning.

FANNY [laughs]. Oh, you poor fellow!

NEWTE. Caught the first train to Melton, and came on by cart. What's the trouble?

FANNY. A good deal. Why didn't you tell me what I was marrying?

NEWTE. I did. I told you that he was a gentleman; that he -

FANNY. Why didn't you tell me that he was Lord Bantock? You knew, didn't you?

NEWTE [begins to see worries ahead]. Can't object to my putting a cigar in my mouth if I don't light it—can he?

FANNY. Oh, light it—anything you like that will help you to get along.

NEWTE [bites the end off the cigar and puts it between his teeth. This helps him]. No, I didn't know—not officially.

FANNY. What do you mean—"not officially"?

NEWTE. He never told me.

FANNY. He never told you ANYTHING—for the matter of that. I understood you had found out everything for yourself.

NEWTE. Yes; and one of the things I found out was that he didn't WANT you to know. I could see his little game. Wanted to play the Lord Burleigh fake. Well, what was the harm? Didn't make any difference to you!

FANNY. Didn't make any difference to me! [Jumps up.] Do you know what I've done? Married into a family that keeps twenty-three servants, every blessed one of whom is a near relation of my own. [He sits paralysed. She goes on.] That bald-headed old owl—[with a wave towards the door]—that wanted to send you off with a glass of beer and a flea in your ear—that's my uncle. The woman that opened the lodge gate for you is my Aunt Amelia. The carroty-headed young man that answered the door to you is my cousin Simeon. He always used to insist on kissing me. I'm expecting him to begin again. My "lady's" maid is my cousin Jane. That's why I'm dressed like this! My own clothes have been packed off to the local dressmaker to be made "decent." Meanwhile, they've dug up the family vault to find something for me to go on with. [He has been fumbling in all his pockets for matches. She snatches a box from somewhere and flings it to him.] For Heaven's sake light it! Then, perhaps, you'll be able to do something else than stare. I have claret and water—mixed— with my dinner. Uncle pours it out for me. They've locked up my cigarettes. Aunt Susannah is coming in to-morrow morning to hear me say my prayers. Doesn't trust me by myself. Thinks I'll skip them. She's the housekeeper here. I've got to know them by heart before I go to bed to-night, and now I've mislaid them. [She goes to the desk—hunts for them.]

NEWTE [having lighted his eternal cigar, he can begin to think]. But why should THEY -

FANNY [still at desk]. Because they're that sort. They honestly think they are doing the right and proper thing—that Providence has put it into their hands to turn me out a passable substitute for all a Lady Bantock should be; which, so far as I can understand, is something between the late lamented Queen Victoria and Goody-Two- Shoes. They are the people that I ran away from, the people I've told you about, the people I've always said I'd rather starve than ever go back to. And here I am, plumped down in the midst of them again—for life! [Honoria Bennet, the "still-room" maid, has entered. She is a pert young minx of about Fanny's own age.] What is is? What is it?

HONORIA. Merely passing through. Sorry to have excited your ladyship. [Goes into dressing-room.]

FANNY. My cousin Honoria. They've sent her up to keep an eye upon me. Little cat! [She takes her handkerchief, drapes it over the keyhole of the dressing-room door.]

NEWTE [at sight of Honoria he has jumped up and hastily hidden his cigar behind him]. What are you going to do?

FANNY [she seats herself and suggests to him the writing-chair].
Hear from you—first of all—exactly what you told Vernon.

NEWTE [sitting]. About you?

FANNY [nods]. About me—and my family.

NEWTE. Well—couldn't tell him much, of course. Wasn't much to tell.

FANNY. I want what you did tell.

NEWTE. I told him that your late father was a musician.

FANNY. Yes.

NEWTE. Had been unfortunate. Didn't go into particulars. Didn't seem to be any need for it. That your mother had died when you were still only a girl and that you had gone to live with relatives. [He looks for approval.]

FANNY. Yes.

NEWTE. That you hadn't got on well with them— artistic temperament, all that sort of thing—that, in consequence, you had appealed to your father's old theatrical friends; and that they—that they, having regard to your talent—and beauty -

FANNY. Thank you.

NEWTE. Had decided that the best thing you could do was to go upon the stage. [He finishes, tolerably well pleased with himself.]

FANNY. That's all right. Very good indeed. What else?

NEWTE [after an uncomfortable pause]. Well, that's about all I knew.

FANNY. Yes, but what did you TELL him?

NEWTE. Well, of course, I had to tell him something. A man doesn't marry without knowing just a little about his wife's connections. Wouldn't be reasonable to expect him. You'd never told me anything— never would; except that you'd liked to have boiled the lot. What was I to do? [He is playing with a quill pen he has picked up.]

FANNY [she takes it from him]. What DID you do?

NEWTE [with fine frankness]. I did the best I could for you, old girl, and he was very nice about it. Said it was better than he'd expected, and that I'd made him very happy—very happy indeed.

FANNY [she leans across, puts her hand on his]. You're a dear, good fellow, George—always have been. I wouldn't plague you only it is absolutely necessary I should know—exactly what you did tell him.

NEWTE [a little sulkily]. I told him that your uncle was a bishop.

FANNY [sits back—staring at him]. A what?

NEWTE. A bishop. Bishop of Waiapu, New Zealand.

FANNY. Why New Zealand?

NEWTE. Why not? Had to be somewhere. Didn't want him Archbishop of Canterbury, did you?

FANNY. Did he believe it?

NEWTE. Shouldn't have told him had there been any fear that he wouldn't.

FANNY. I see. Any other swell relations of mine knocking about?

NEWTE. One—a judge of the Supreme Court in Ohio. Same name, anyhow, O'Gorman. Thought I'd make him a cousin of yours. I've always remembered him. Met him when I was over there in ninety- eight—damn him!

[A silence.]

FANNY [she rises]. Well, nothing else for it! Got to tell him it was all a pack of lies. Not blaming you, old boy— my fault. Didn't know he was going to ask any questions, or I'd have told him myself. Bit of bad luck, that's all.

NEWTE. Why must you tell him? Only upset him.

FANNY. It's either my telling him or leaving it for them to do. You know me, George. How long do you see me being bossed and bullied by my own servants? Besides, it's bound to come out in any case.

NEWTE [he rises. Kindly but firmly he puts her back into her chair. Then pacing to and fro with his hands mostly in his trousers pockets, he talks]. Now, you listen to me, old girl. I've been your business manager ever since you started in. I've never made a mistake before- - [he turns and faces her]—and I haven't made one this time.

FANNY. I don't really see the smartness, George, stuffing him up with a lot of lies he can find out for himself.

NEWTE. IF HE WANTS TO. A couple of telegrams, one to His Grace the Bishop of Waiapu, the other to Judge Denis O'Gorman, Columbus, Ohio, would have brought him back the information that neither gentlemen had ever heard of you. IF HE HADN'T BEEN CAREFUL NOT TO SEND THEM. He wasn't marrying you with the idea of strengthening his family connections. He was marrying you because he was just gone on you. Couldn't help himself.

FANNY. In that case, you might just as well have told him the truth.

NEWTE. WHICH HE WOULD THEN HAVE HAD TO PASS ON TO EVERYONE ENTITLED TO ASK QUESTIONS. Can't you understand? Somebody, in the interest of everybody, had to tell a lie. Well, what's a business manager for?

FANNY. But I can't do it, George. You don't know them. The longer I give in to them the worse they'll get.

NEWTE. Can't you square them?

FANNY. No, that's the trouble. They ARE honest. They're the "faithful retainers" out of a melodrama. They are working eighteen hours a day on me not for any advantage to themselves, but because they think it their "duty" to the family. They don't seem to have any use for themselves at all.

NEWTE. Well, what about the boy? Can't HE talk to them?

FANNY. Vernon! They've brought him up from a baby—spanked him all round, I expect. Might as well ask a boy to talk to his old schoolmaster. Besides, if he did talk, then it would all come out. As I tell you, it's bound to come out—and the sooner the better.

NEWTE. It must NOT come out! It's too late. If we had told him at the beginning that he was proposing to marry into his own butler's family—well, it's an awkward situation—he might have decided to risk it. Or he might have cried off.

FANNY. And a good job if he had.

NEWTE. Now talk sense. You wanted him—you took a fancy to him from the beginning. He's a nice boy, and there's something owing to him. [It is his trump card, and he knows it.] Don't forget that. He's been busy, explaining to all his friends and relations why they should receive you with open arms: really nice girl, born gentlewoman, good old Church of England family—no objection possible. For you to spring the truth upon him NOW—well, it doesn't seem to me quite fair to HIM.

FANNY. Then am I to live all my life dressed as a charity girl?

NEWTE. You keep your head and things will gradually right themselves. This family of yours—they've got SOME sense, I suppose?

FANNY. Never noticed any sign of it myself.

NEWTE. Maybe you're not a judge. [Laughs.] They'll listen to reason. You let ME have a talk to them, one of these days; see if I can't show them—first one and then the other—the advantage of leaving to "better" themselves—WITH THE HELP OF A LITTLE READY MONEY. Later on—choosing your proper time—you can break it to him that you have discovered they're distant connections of yours, a younger branch of the family that you'd forgotten. Give the show time to settle down into a run. Then you can begin to make changes.

FANNY. You've a wonderful way with you, George. It always sounds right as you put it—even when one jolly well knows that it isn't.

NEWTE. Well, it's always been right for you, old girl, ain't it?

FANNY. Yes. You've been a rattling good friend. [She takes his hands.] Almost wish I'd married you instead. We'd have been more suited to one another.

NEWTE [shakes his head]. Nothing like having your fancy. You'd never have been happy without him. [He releases her.] 'Twas a good engagement, or I'd never have sanctioned it.

FANNY. I suppose it will be the last one you will ever get me. [She has dropped for a moment into a brown study.]

NEWTE [he turns]. I hope so.

FANNY [she throws off her momentary mood with a laugh]. Poor fellow! You never even got your commission.

NEWTE. I'll take ten per cent. of all your happiness, old girl. So make it as much as you can for my benefit. Good-bye. [He holds out hand.]

FANNY. You're not going? You'll stop to lunch?

NEWTE. Not to-day.

FANNY. Do. If you don't, they'll think it's because I was frightened to ask you.

NEWTE. All the better. The more the other party thinks he's having his way, the easier always to get your own. Your trouble is, you know, that you never had any tact.

FANNY. I hate tact. [Newte laughs.] We could have had such a jolly little lunch together. I'm all alone till the evening. There were ever so many things I wanted to talk to you about.

NEWTE. What?

FANNY. Ah, how can one talk to a man with his watch in his hand? [He puts it away and stands waiting, but she is cross.] I think you're very disagreeable.

NEWTE. I must really get back to town. I oughtn't to be away now, only your telegram -

FANNY. I know. I'm an ungrateful little beast! [She crosses and rings bell.] You'll have a glass of champagne before you go?

NEWTE. Well, I won't say no to that.

FANNY. How are all the girls?

NEWTE. Oh, chirpy. I'm bringing them over to London. We open at the Palace next week.

FANNY. What did they think of my marriage? Gerty was a bit jealous, wasn't she?

NEWTE. Well, would have been, if she'd known who he was. [Laughs.]

FANNY. Tell her. Tell her [she draws herself up] I'm Lady Bantock, of Bantock Hall, Rutlandshire. It will make her so mad. [Laughs.]

NEWTE [laughs]. I will.

FANNY. Give them all my love. [Ernest appears in answer to her bell.] Oh, Ernest, tell Bennet—[the eyes and mouth of Ernest open]- -to see that Mr. Newte has some refreshment before he leaves. A glass of champagne and—and some caviare. Don't forget. [Ernest goes out.] Good-bye. You'll come again?

NEWTE. Whenever you want me—and remember—the watchword is "Tact"!

FANNY. Yes, I've got the WORD all right. [Laughs.] Don't forget to give my love to the girls.

NEWTE. I won't. So long! [He goes out.]

Fanny closes the door. Honoria has re-entered from the dressing- room. She looks from the handkerchief still hanging over the keyhole to Fanny.

HONORIA. Your ladyship's handkerchief?

FANNY. Yes. Such a draught through that keyhole.

HONORIA [takes the handkerchief, hands it to Fanny]. I will tell the housekeeper.

FANNY. Thanks. Maybe you will also mention it to the butler. Possibly also to the—[She suddenly changes.] Honoria. Suppose it had been you—you know, you're awfully pretty—who had married Lord Bantock, and he had brought you back here, among them all—uncle, aunt, all the lot of them—what would you have done?

HONORIA [she draws herself up]. I should have made it quite plain from the first, that I was mistress, and that they were my servants.

FANNY. You would, you think -

HONORIA [checking her outburst]. But then, dear—
you will excuse my speaking plainly—there is a slight
difference between the two cases. [She seats herself on
the settee. Fanny is standing near the desk.] You see,
what we all feel about you, dear, is—that you are—well,
hardly a fit wife for his lordship. [Fanny's hands are
itching to box the girl's ears. To save herself, she grinds
out through her teeth the word "Tack!"] Of course, dear,
it isn't altogether your fault.

FANNY. Thanks.

HONORIA. Your mother's marriage was most
unfortunate.

FANNY [her efforts to suppress her feelings are just—
but only just— successful.] Need we discuss that?

HONORIA. Well, he was an Irishman, dear, there's no
denying it. [Fanny takes a cushion from a chair—with
her back to Honoria, she strangles it. Jane has entered
and is listening.] Still, perhaps it is a painful subject. And
we hope—all of us—that, with time and patience, we
may succeed in eradicating the natural results of your
bringing-up.

JANE. Some families, finding themselves in our position,
would seek to turn it to their own advantage. WE think
only of your good.

FANNY. Yes, that's what I feel—that you are worrying yourselves too much about me. You're too conscientious, all of you. You, in particular, Jane, because you know you're not strong. YOU'LL end up with a nervous breakdown. [Mrs. Bennet has entered. Honoria slips out. Fanny turns to her aunt.] I was just saying how anxious I'm getting about Jane. I don't like the look of her at all. What she wants is a holiday. Don't you agree with me?

MRS. BENNET. There will be no holiday, I fear, for any of us, for many a long day.

FANNY. But you must. You must think more of yourselves, you know. YOU'RE not looking well, aunt, at all. What you both want is a month—at the seaside.

MRS. BENNET. Your object is too painfully apparent for the subject to need discussion. True solicitude for us would express itself better in greater watchfulness upon your own behaviour.

FANNY. Why, what have I done?

[Bennet enters, followed, unwillingly, by Ernest.]

MRS. BENNET. Your uncle will explain.

BENNET. Shut that door. [Ernest does so. They group round Bennet— Ernest a little behind. Fanny remains near the desk.] Sit down. [Fanny, bewildered, speechless, sits.] Carry your mind back, please, to the moment when, with the Bradshaw in front of you, you were considering, with the help of your cousin Ernest, the possibility of your slipping out unobserved, to meet and commune with a person you had surreptitiously summoned to visit you during your husband's absence.

FANNY. While I think of it, did he have anything to eat before he went? I told Ernest to—ask you to see that he had a glass of champagne and a -

BENNET [waves her back into silence]. Mr. Newte was given refreshment suitable to his station. [She goes to interrupt. Again he waves her back.] We are speaking of more important matters. Your cousin reminded you that you would have to pass the lodge, occupied by your Aunt Amelia. I state the case correctly?

FANNY. Beautifully!

BENNET. I said nothing at the time, doubting the evidence of my own ears. The boy, however—where is the boy?—[Ernest is pushed forward]—has admitted—reluctantly—that he also heard it. [A pause. The solemnity deepens.] You made use of an expression -

FANNY. Oh, cut it short. I said "damn." [A shudder passes.] I'm sorry to have frightened you, but if you knew a little more of really good society, you would know that ladies—quite slap-up ladies—when they're excited, do—.

MRS. BENNET [interrupting with almost a scream]. She defends it!

BENNET. You will allow ME to be the judge of what a LADY says, even when she is excited. As for this man, Newte -

FANNY. The best friend you ever had. [She is "up" again.] You thank your stars, all of you, and tell the others, too, the whole blessed twenty-three of you—you thank your stars that I did "surreptitiously" beg and pray him to run down by the first train and have a talk with me; and that Providence was kind enough to YOU to enable him to come. It's a very different tune you'd have been singing at this moment—all of you—if he hadn't. I can tell you that.

MRS. BENNET. And pray, what tune SHOULD we have been singing if Providence hadn't been so thoughtful of us?

FANNY [she is about to answer, then checks herself, and sits again]. You take care you don't find out. There's time yet.

MRS. BENNET. We had better leave her.

BENNET. Threats, my good girl, will not help you.

MRS. BENNET [with a laugh]. She's in too tight a corner for that.

BENNET. A contrite heart is what your aunt and I desire to see. [He takes from his pocket a small book, places it open on the desk.] I have marked one or two passages, on pages 93-7. We will discuss them together— later in the day.

They troop out in silence, the key turns in the lock.

FANNY [takes up the book—turns to the cover, reads]. "The Sinner's Manual." [She turns to page 93.]

[CURTAIN]

ACT III

SCENE

The same.

Time.—A few days later.

[A table is laid for tea. Ernest enters with the tea-urn. He leaves the door open; through it comes the sound of an harmonium, accompanying the singing of a hymn. Fanny comes from her dressing- room. She is dressed more cheerfully than when we last saw her, but still "seemly." She has a book in her hand. She pauses, hearing the music, goes nearer to the open door, and listens; then crosses and takes her place at the table. The music ceases.]

FANNY. Another prayer meeting? [Ernest nods.] I do keep 'em busy.

ERNEST. D'ye know what they call you downstairs?

FANNY. What?

ERNEST. The family cross.

FANNY. I'm afraid it's about right.

ERNEST. What have you been doing THIS time? Swearing again?

FANNY. Worse. I've been lying. [Ernest gives vent to a low whistle.] Said I didn't know what had become of that yellow poplin with the black lace flounces, that they've had altered for me. Found out that I'd given it to old Mother Potts for the rummage sale at the Vicarage. Jane was down there. Bought it in for half a crown.

ERNEST. You are risky. Why, you might have known -

[Vernon comes in. He is in golfing get-up. He throws his cap on to the settee.]

VERNON. Hello, got a cup of tea there?

[Ernest goes out.]

FANNY. Yes. Thought you were playing golf?

VERNON. Just had a telegram handed to me in the village—from your friend Newte. Wants me to meet him at Melton Station at five o'clock. [Looks at his watch.] Know what he wants?

FANNY. Haven't the faintest idea. [She hands him his cup.] Is he coming HERE? Or merely on his way somewhere?

VERNON. I don't know; he doesn't say.

FANNY. Don't let him mix you up in any of his "ventures." Dear old George, he's as honest as the day, but if he gets hold of an "idea" there's always thousands in it for everybody.

VERNON. I'll be careful. [Ernest has left the door open. The harmonium breaks forth again, together with vocal accompaniment as before.] What's on downstairs, then—a party?

FANNY. Bennet is holding a prayer meeting.

VERNON. A prayer meeting?

FANNY. One of the younger members of the family has been detected "telling a deliberate lie." [Vernon is near the door listening, with his back towards her, or he would see that she is smiling.] Black sheep, I suppose, to be found in every flock. [Music ceases, Ernest having arrived with the news of his lordship's return.]

VERNON [returning to the table, having closed the door]. Good old man, you know, Bennet. All of them! So high-principled! Don't often get servants like that, nowadays.

FANNY. Seems almost selfish, keeping the whole collection to ourselves.

VERNON [laughs]. 'Pon my word it does. But what can we do? They'll never leave us—not one of them.

FANNY. No, I don't believe they ever will.

VERNON. Do you know, I sometimes think that you don't like them. [Fanny makes a movement.] Of course, they are a bit bossy, I admit. But all that comes from their devotion, their -

FANNY. The wonder to me is that, brought up among them, admiring them as you do, you never thought of marrying one of them.

VERNON [staggered.] Marrying them?

FANNY. I didn't say "them." I said "ONE of them." There's Honoria. She's pretty enough, anyhow. So's Alice, Charles Bennet's daughter, and Bertha and Grace—all of them beautiful. And what's even better still—good. [She says it viciously.] Didn't you ever think of them?

VERNON. Well [laughs]—well, one hardly marries into one's own kitchen.

FANNY. Isn't that rather snobbish? You say they're more like friends than servants. They've lived with your people, side by side, for three generations, doing their duty, honourably. There's never been a slur upon their name. They're "high-principled." You know it. They've better manners than nine-tenths of your smart society, and they're healthy. What's wrong with them—even from a lord's point of view?

VERNON [recovering himself]. Well, don't pitch into me about it. It's your fault if I didn't marry them—I mean one of them. [He laughs, puts his empty cup back on the table.] Maybe I'd have thought about it—if I hadn't met you.

FANNY [takes his hand in hers]. I wish you hadn't asked Newte any questions about me. It would have been so nice to feel that you had married me—just because you couldn't help it—just because I was I and nothing else mattered.

VERNON. Let's forget I ever did. [He kneels beside her.] I didn't do it for my own sake, as you know. A MAN in my position has to think of other people. His wife has to take her place in society. People insist upon knowing something about her. It's not enough for the stupid "County" that she's the cleverest, most bewilderingly beautiful, bewitching lady in the land.

FANNY. And how long will you think all that?

VERNON. For ever, and ever, and ever.

FANNY. Oh, you dear boy. [She kisses him.] You don't know how a woman loves the man she loves to love her. [Laughs.] Isn't that complicated?

VERNON. Not at all. We're just the same. We love to love the woman we love.

FANNY. Provided the "County" will let us. And the County has said: A man may not marry his butler's niece.

VERNON [laughing]. You've got butlers on the brain. If ever I do run away with my own cook or under-housemaid, it will be your doing.

FANNY. You haven't the pluck! The "County" would laugh at you. You men are so frightened of being laughed at.

VERNON [he rises]. Well, if it saves us from making asses of ourselves -

FANNY. Wasn't there a niece of old Bennet's, a girl who had been brought up abroad, and who WASN'T a domestic servant—never had been- -who stayed with them here, at the gardener's cottage, for a short time, some few years ago?

VERNON. You mean poor Rose Bennet's daughter— the one who ran away and married an organ-grinder.

FANNY. An organ-grinder?

VERNON. Something of that sort—yes. They had her over; did all they could. A crazy sort of girl; used to sing French ballads on the village green to all the farm labourers she could collect. Shortened poor Bennet's life by about ten years. [Laughs.] But why? Not going to bully me for not having fallen in love with her, are you? Because that really WASN'T my fault. I never even saw her. 'Twas the winter we spent in Rome. She bolted before we got back. Never gave me a chance.

FANNY. I accept the excuse. [Laughs.] No, I was merely wondering what the "County" would have done if by any chance you had married HER. Couldn't have said you were marrying into your own kitchen in her case, because she was never IN your kitchen—absolutely refused to enter it, I'm told.

VERNON [laughs]. It would have been a "nice point," as they say in legal circles. If people had liked her, they'd have tried to forget that her cousins had ever been scullery-maids. If not, they'd have taken good care that nobody did.

[Bennet enters. He brings some cut flowers, with the "placing" of which he occupies himself.]

BENNET. I did not know your lordship had returned.

VERNON. Found a telegram waiting for me in the village. What's become of that niece of yours, Bennet— your sister Rose's daughter, who was here for a short time and ran away again? Ever hear anything about her?

BENNET [very quietly he turns, lets his eyes for a moment meet Fanny's. Then answers as he crosses to the windows]. The last I heard about her was that she was married.

VERNON. Satisfactorily?

BENNET. Looking at it from her point of view—most satisfactorily.

VERNON [laughs]. But looking at it from his—more doubtful?

BENNET. She was not without her attractions. Her chief faults, I am inclined to think, were those arising from want of discipline in youth. I have hopes that it is not even yet too late to root out from her nature the weeds of indiscretion.

VERNON. And you think he is the man to do it?

BENNET. Perhaps not. But fortunately there are those about her fully alive to the duty devolving upon them.

VERNON. Um. Sounds a little bit like penal servitude for the poor girl, the way you put it, Bennet.

BENNET. Even penal servitude may be a blessing, if it serves to correct a stubborn spirit.

VERNON. We'll have to make you a J.P., Bennet. Must be jolly careful I don't ever get tried before you. [Laughs.] Is that the cart?

BENNET [he looks out through the window]. Yes, your lordship.

VERNON [he takes up his cap]. I may be bringing someone back with me. [To Fanny, who throughout has remained seated.] Why not put on your hat—come with me?

FANNY [she jumps up, delighted]. Shall I?

BENNET. Your ladyship is not forgetting that to-day is Wednesday?

FANNY. What's the odds. There's nobody to call. Everybody is still in town.

BENNET. It has always been the custom of the Lady Bantocks, when in residence, to be at home on Wednesdays.

VERNON. Perhaps better not. It may cause talk; if, by chance, anybody does come. I was forgetting it was Wednesday. [Fanny sits again.] I shan't do anything without consulting you. Good-bye.

FANNY. Good-bye.

[Vernon goes out.]

BENNET. You think it wise, discussing with his lordship the secret history of the Bennet family?

FANNY. What do you mean by telling him my father was an organ- grinder? If the British public knew the difference between music and a hurdy-gurdy, he would have kept a butler of his own.

BENNET. I am not aware of having mentioned to his lordship that you ever to my knowledge even had a father. It is not my plan—for the present at all events—to inform his lordship anything about your family. Take care I am not forced to.

FANNY. Because my father, a composer who had his work performed at the Lamoureux Concerts—as I can prove, because I've got the programme—had the misfortune to marry into a family of lackeys—I'm not talking about my mother: she was never really one of you. SHE had the soul of an artist.

BENNET [white with suppressed fury; he is in front of her; his very look is enough to silence her]. Now you listen to me, my girl, once and for all. I told you the night of your arrival that whether this business was going to prove a pleasant or an unpleasant one depended upon you. You make it an easy one—for your own sake. With one word I can bring your house of cards about your ears. I've only to tell him the truth for him to know you as a cheat and liar. [She goes to speak; again he silences her.] You listen to me. You've seen fit to use strong language; now I'm using strong language. This BOY, who has married you in a moment of impulse, what does HE know about the sort of wife a man in his position needs? What do YOU? made to sing for your living on the Paris boulevards—whose only acquaintance with the upper classes has been at shady restaurants.

FANNY. He didn't WANT a woman of his own class. He told me so. It was because I wasn't a colourless, conventional puppet with a book of etiquette in place of a soul that he was first drawn towards me.

BENNET. Yes. At twenty-two, boys like unconventionality. Men don't: they've learnt its true name, vulgarity. Do you think I've stood behind English society for forty years without learning anything about it! What you call a colourless puppet is what WE call an English lady. And that you've got to learn to be. You talk of "lackeys." If your mother, my poor sister Rose, came from a family of "lackeys" there would be no hope for you. With her blood in your veins the thing can be done. We Bennets—[he draws himself up]—we serve. We are not lackeys.

FANNY. All right. Don't you call my father an organ-grinder, and I won't call you lackeys. Unfortunately that doesn't end the trouble.

BENNET. The trouble can easily be ended.

FANNY. Yes. By my submitting to be ruled in all things for the remainder of my life by my own servants.

BENNET. Say "relations," and it need not sound so unpleasant.

FANNY. Yes, it would. It would sound worse. One can get rid of one's servants. [She has crossed towards the desk. Her cheque-book lies there half hidden under other papers. It catches her eye. Her hand steals unconsciously towards it. She taps it idly with her fingers. It is all the work of a moment. Nothing comes of it. Just the idea passes through her brain—not for the first time. She does nothing noticeable—merely stands listless while one might count half a dozen—then turns to him again.] Don't you think you're going it a bit too strong, all of you? I'm not a fool. I've got a lot to learn, I know. I'd be grateful for help. What you're trying to do is to turn me into a new woman entirely.

BENNET. Because that is the only WAY to help you. Men do not put new wine into old bottles.

FANNY. Oh, don't begin quoting Scripture. I want to discuss the thing sensibly. Don't you see it can't be done? I can't be anybody else than myself. I don't want to.

BENNET. My girl, you've GOT to be. Root and branch, inside and outside, before you're fit to be Lady Bantock, mother of the Lord Bantocks that are to be, you've got to be a changed woman.

[A pause.]

FANNY. And it's going to be your job, from beginning to end—yours and the rest of you. What I wear and how I look is Jane's affair. My prayers will be for what Aunt Susannah thinks I stand in need of. What I eat and drink and say and do YOU will arrange for me. And when you die, Cousin Simeon, I suppose, will take your place. And when Aunt Susannah dies, it will merely be a change to Aunt Amelia. And if Jane ever dies, Honoria will have the dressing and the lecturing of me. And so on and so on, world without end, for ever and ever, Amen.

BENNET. Before that time, you will, I shall hope, have learnt sufficient sense to be grateful to us. [He goes out.]

FANNY [she turns—walks slowly back towards the tea-table. Halfway she pauses, and leaning over the back of a chair regards in silence for a while the portrait of the first Lady Bantock]. I do wish I could tell what you were saying.

[The door opens. The Misses Wetherell come in. They wear the same frocks that they wore in the first act. They pause. Fanny is still gazing at the portrait.]

THE ELDER MISS WETHERELL. Don't you notice it, dear?

THE YOUNGER MISS WETHERELL. Yes. There really is.

THE ELDER MISS WETHERELL. It struck me the first day. [To Fanny, who has turned] Your likeness, dear, to Lady Constance. It's really quite remarkable.

FANNY. You think so?

THE YOUNGER MISS WETHERELL. It's your expression—when you are serious.

FANNY [laughs]. I must try to be more serious.

THE ELDER MISS WETHERELL. It will come, dear.

[They take their places side by side on the settee.]

THE YOUNGER MISS WETHERELL [to her sister, with a pat of the hand]. In good time. It's so nice to have her young. I wonder if anybody'll come this afternoon.

THE ELDER MISS WETHERELL [to Fanny]. You see, dear, most of the county people are still in town.

FANNY [who is pouring out tea]. I'm not grumbling.

THE ELDER MISS WETHERELL. Oh, you'll like them, dear. The Cracklethorpes especially. [To her sister for confirmation] Bella Cracklethorpe is so clever.

THE YOUNGER MISS WETHERELL. And the Engells. She'll like the Engells. All the Engell girls are so pretty. [Fanny brings over two cups of tea.] Thank you, dear.

THE ELDER MISS WETHERELL [as she takes her cup—patting Fanny's hand]. And they'll like you, dear, ALL of them.

FANNY [returning to table]. I hope so.

THE ELDER MISS WETHERELL. It's wonderful, dear—you won't mind my saying it?—how you've improved.

THE YOUNGER MISS WETHERELL. Of course it was such a change for you. And at first [turns to her sister] we were a little anxious about her, weren't we?

[Fanny has returned to them with the cake-basket.]

THE ELDER MISS WETHERELL [as she takes a piece]. Bennet [she lingers on the name as that of an authority] was saying only yesterday that he had great hopes of you.

THE YOUNGER MISS WETHERELL [Fanny is handing the basket to her]. Thank you, dear.

THE ELDER MISS WETHERELL. I told Vernon. He was SO pleased.

FANNY. VERNON was?

THE ELDER MISS WETHERELL. He attaches so much importance to Bennet's opinion.

FANNY. Um. I'm glad I appear to be giving satisfaction. [She has returned to her seat at the table.] I suppose when you go to town, you take the Bennets with you?

THE ELDER MISS WETHERELL [surprised at the question]. Of course, dear.

THE YOUNGER MISS WETHERELL. Vernon didn't wish to go this year. He thought you would prefer -

FANNY. I was merely thinking of when he did. Do you ever go abroad for the winter? So many people do, nowadays.

THE ELDER MISS WETHERELL. We tried it once. But there was nothing for dear Vernon to do. You see, he's so fond of hunting.

THE YOUNGER MISS WETHERELL [to her sister]. And then there will be his Parliamentary duties that he will have to take up now.

[Fanny rises, abruptly.]

THE ELDER MISS WETHERELL. You're not ill, dear?

FANNY. No. Merely felt I wanted some air. You don't mind, do you? [She flings a casement open.]

THE YOUNGER MISS WETHERELL. Not at all, dear. [To her sister] It IS a bit close.

THE ELDER MISS WETHERELL. One could really do without fires.

THE YOUNGER MISS WETHERELL. If it wasn't for the evenings.

THE ELDER MISS WETHERELL. And then, of course, the cold weather might come again. One can never feel safe until -

[The door opens. Dr. Freemantle enters, announced by Bennet. The old ladies go to rise. He stops them.]

DR. FREEMANTLE. Don't get up. [He shakes hands with them.] How are we this afternoon? [He shakes his head and clicks his tongue.] Really, I think I shall have to bring an action for damages against Lady Bantock. Ever since she -

THE ELDER MISS WETHERELL. Hush! [She points to the window.] Fanny.

THE YOUNGER MISS WETHERELL. Here's Doctor Freemantle.

[Fanny comes from the window.]

DR. FREEMANTLE [he meets her and takes her hand]. Was just saying, I really think I shall have to claim damages against you, Lady Bantock. You've practically deprived me of two of my best paying patients. Used to be sending for me every other day before you came. Now look at them! [The two ladies laugh.] She's not as bad as we expected. [He pats her hand.] Do you remember my description of what I thought she was going to be like?

THE YOUNGER MISS WETHERELL. She's a dear girl.

THE ELDER MISS WETHERELL. Bennet -

FANNY [she has crossed to table—is pouring out the Doctor's tea]. Oh, mightn't we have a holiday from Bennet?

DR. FREEMANTLE [laughs]. Seems to be having a holiday himself to- day.

THE YOUNGER MISS WETHERELL. A holiday?

DR. FREEMANTLE. Didn't you know? Oh, there's an awfully swagger party on downstairs. They were all trooping in as I came.

THE YOUNGER MISS WETHERELL. I'd no idea he was giving a party. [To Fanny] Did you, dear?

FANNY [she hands the Doctor his tea]. Yes. It's a prayer meeting. The whole family, I expect, has been summoned.

DR. FREEMANTLE. A prayer meeting! Didn't look like it.

THE ELDER MISS WETHERELL. But why should he be holding a prayer meeting?

FANNY. Oh, one of the family -

DR. FREEMANTLE. And why twelve girls in a van?

THE YOUNGER MISS WETHERELL. In a van?

DR. FREEMANTLE. One of Hutton's from the Station Hotel—with a big poster pinned on the door: "Our Empire."

[Fanny has risen. She crosses and rings the bell.]

THE YOUNGER MISS WETHERELL. What's the matter, dear?

FANNY. I'm not quite sure yet. [Her whole manner is changed. A look has come into her eyes that has not been there before. She speaks in quiet, determined tones. She rings again. Then returning to table, hands the cake-basket to the Doctor.] Won't you take one, Doctor? They're not as indigestible as they look. [Laughs.]

DR. FREEMANTLE [he also is bewildered at the changed atmosphere]. Thank you. I hope I -

FANNY [she turns to Ernest, who has entered. Her tone, for the first time, is that of a mistress speaking to her servants]. Have any visitors called for me this afternoon?

ERNEST. Vi-visitors—?

FANNY. Some ladies.

ERNEST [he is in a slough of doubt and terror]. L— ladies?

FANNY. Yes. Please try to understand the English language. Has a party of ladies called here this afternoon?

ERNEST. There have been some ladies. They—we -

FANNY. Where are they?

ERNEST. They—I -

FANNY. Send Bennet up to me. Instantly, please.

[Ernest, only too glad to be off, stumbles out.]

THE YOUNGER MISS WETHERELL. My dear -

FANNY. You'll take some more tea, won't you? Do you mind, Doctor, passing Miss Wetherell's cup? And the other one. Thank you. And will you pass them the biscuits? You see, I am doing all I can on your behalf. [She is talking and laughing—a little hysterically— for the purpose of filling time.] Tea and hot cake—could anything be worse for them?

DR. FREEMANTLE. Well, tea, you know -

FANNY. I know. [Laughs.] You doctors are all alike. You all denounce it, but you all drink it. [She hands him the two cups.] That one is for Aunt Wetherell of the beautiful hair; and the other is for Aunt Wetherell of the beautiful eyes. [Laughs.] It's the only way I can distinguish them.

[Bennet enters.]

Oh, Bennet!

BENNET. You sent for me?

FANNY. Yes. I understand some ladies have called.

BENNET. I think your ladyship must have been misinformed. I most certainly have seen none.

FANNY. I have to assume, Bennet, that either Dr. Freemantle or you are telling lies.

[A silence.]

BENNET. A party of over-dressed young women, claiming to be acquainted with your ladyship, have arrived in a van. I am giving them tea in the servants' hall, and will see to it that they are sent back to the station in ample time to catch their train back to town.

FANNY. Please show them up. They will have their tea here.

BENNET [her very quietness is beginning to alarm him. It shakes him from his customary perfection of manners]. The Lady Bantocks do not as a rule receive circus girls in their boudoir.

FANNY [still with her alarming quietness]. Neither do they argue with their servants. Please show these ladies in.

BENNET. I warn you -

FANNY. You heard my orders. [Her tone has the right ring. The force of habit is too strong upon him. He yields—savagely—and goes out. She turns to the Doctor.] So sorry I had to drag you into it. I didn't see how else I was going to floor him.

DR. FREEMANTLE. Splendid! [He grips her hand.]

FANNY [she goes to the old ladies who sit bewildered terrified.] They won't be here for more than a few minutes—they can't be. I want you to be nice to them— both of you. They are friends of mine. [She turns to the Doctor.] They're the girls I used to act with. We went all over Europe—twelve of us—representing the British Empire. They are playing in London now.

DR. FREEMANTLE. To-night? [He looks at his watch.]

FANNY [she is busy at the tea-table]. Yes. They are on the stage at half past nine. You might look out their train for them. [She points to the Bradshaw on the desk.] I don't suppose they've ever thought about how they're going to get back. It's Judy's inspiration, this, the whole thing; I'd bet upon it. [With a laugh.] She always was as mad as a March hare.

DR. FREEMANTLE [busy with the Bradshaw]. They were nice-looking girls.

FANNY. Yes. I think we did the old man credit. [With a laugh.]
John Bull's daughters, they called us in Paris.

[Bennet appears in doorway.]

BENNET [announces]. "Our Empire."

[Headed by "England," the twelve girls, laughing, crowding, jostling one another, talking all together, swoop in.]

ENGLAND [a lady with a decided Cockney accent]. Oh, my dear, talk about an afternoon! We 'ave 'ad a treat getting 'ere.

[Fanny kisses her.]

SCOTLAND [they also kiss]. Your boss told us you'd gone out.

FANNY. It was a slight—misunderstanding. Bennet, take away these things, please. And let me have half a dozen bottles of champagne.

STRAITS SETTLEMENTS [a small girl at the back of the crowd—with a shrill voice]. Hooray!

BENNET [he is controlling himself with the supremest difficulty. Within he is a furnace]. I'm afraid I have mislaid the key of the cellar.

FANNY [she looks at him]. You will please find it— quickly. [Bennet, again from habit, yields. But his control almost fails him. He takes up the tray of unneeded tea-things from the table.] I shall want some more of all these [cakes, fruit, sandwiches, etc.]. And some people to wait. Tell Jane she must come and help.

[Bennet goes out. During this passage of arms between mistress and man a momentary lull has taken place in the hubbub. As he goes out, it begins to grow again.]

ENGLAND. 'E does tease yer, don't 'e? Wanted us to 'ave tea in the kitchen.

FANNY. Yes. These old family servants -

AFRICA [she prides herself on being "quite the lady"]. Don't talk about 'em, dear. We had just such another. [She turns to a girl near her.] Oh, they'll run the whole show for you if you let 'em.

ENGLAND. It was Judy's idea, our giving you this little treat. Don't you blime me for it.

WALES [a small, sprightly girl with a childish, laughing voice]. Well, we were all together with nothing better to do. They'd called a rehearsal and then found they didn't want us—silly fools. I told 'em you'd just be tickled to death.

FANNY [laughing—kisses her]. So I am. It was a brilliant idea. [By this time she has kissed or shaken hands with the whole dozen.] I can't introduce you all singly; it would take too long. [She makes a wholesale affair of it.] My aunts, the Misses Wetherell—Dr. Freemantle.

[The Misses Wetherell, suggesting two mice being introduced to a party of friendly kittens, standing, clinging to one another, murmur something inaudible.]

DR. FREEMANTLE [who is with them to comfort them—he has got rid of the time-table, discreetly—smiles]. Delighted.

ENGLAND. Charmed. [The others join in, turning it into a chorus. To Fanny] Glad we didn't strike one of your busy days. I say, you're not as dressy as you used to be. 'Ow are they doing you?—all right?

FANNY. Yes. Oh, yes.

CANADA ["Gerty," a big, handsome girl, with a loud, commanding voice]. George gave me your message.

FANNY [puzzled at first]. My message? [Remembering—laughs.] Oh. That I was Lady Bantock of Bantock Hall. Yes. I thought you'd be pleased.

CANADA. Was delighted, dear.

FANNY. So glad.

CANADA. I'd always had the idea that you were going to make a mess of your marriage.

FANNY. What a funny idea! [But the laugh that accompanies it is not a merry one.]

CANADA. Wasn't it? So glad I was wrong.

WALES. We're all of us looking out for lords in disguise, now. Can't you give us a tip, dear, how to tell 'em?

SCOTLAND. Sukey has broken it off with her boy. Found he was mixed up in trade.

STRAITS SETTLEMENTS [as before, unseen at back of crowd]. No. I didn't. 'Twas his moral character.

[Then enter Honoria with glasses on a tray; Ernest with champagne; Jane with eatables; Bennet with a napkin. It is a grim procession. The girls are scattered, laughing, talking: Africa to the Misses Wetherell; a couple to Dr. Freemantle. England, Scotland, Wales, and Canada are with Fanny. The hubbub, with the advent of the refreshments, increases. There is a general movement towards the refreshments.]

FANNY. Thanks, Bennet. You can clear away a corner of the desk.

ENGLAND [aside to her]. Go easy with it, dear. [Fanny, smiling, nods. She directs operations in a low tone to the Bennets, who take her orders in grim silence and with lips tight shut.] Don't forget, girls, that we've got to get back to-night. [Aside to the Doctor, who has come forward to help.] Some of 'em, you know, ain't used to it.

DR. FREEMANTLE [nods]. Glasses not TOO full. [He whispers to Fanny.]

IRELAND [a decided young woman]. How much time have we got?

ENGLAND. Don't ask me. It's Judy's show.

WALES [mimicking Newte]. The return train, ladies, leaves Oakham station. [Stops—she is facing the clock. She begins to laugh.]

ENGLAND. What's the matter?

WALES [still laughing]. We've got just quarter of an hour to catch it.

[There is a wild rush for the refreshments. Jane is swept off her feet. Bennet's tray is upset.]

ENGLAND. Quarter—! Oh, my Gawd! Here, tuck up your skirts, girls. We'll have to -

DR. FREEMANTLE. It's all right. You've got plenty of time, ladies. There's a train from Norton on the branch line at 5.33. Gets you into London at a quarter to nine.

ENGLAND. You're SURE?

DR. FREEMANTLE [he has his watch in his hand]. Quite sure. The station is only half a mile away.

ENGLAND. Don't let's miss it. Keep your watch in your 'and, there's a dear.

FANNY [her business is—and has been—to move quietly through the throng, making the girls welcome, talking, laughing with them, directing the servants—all in a lady's way. On the whole she does it remarkably well. She is offering a plate of fruit to Judy]. You're a nice acting manager, you are. [Judy laughs. Fanny finds herself in front of Ireland. She turns to England.] Won't you introduce us?

ENGLAND. I beg your pardon, dear. Of course, you don't know each other. Miss Tetsworth, our new Ireland, Lady Bantock. It is "Bantock," isn't it, dear?

FANNY. Quite right. It's a good little part, isn't it?

IRELAND. Well, depends upon what you've been used to.

ENGLAND. She's got talent, as I tell 'er. But she ain't you, dear. It's no good saying she is.

FANNY [hastening to smooth it over]. People always speak so well of us after we're gone. [Laughs.] You'll take another glass of champagne.

IRELAND. Thank you—you made a great success, they tell me, in the part.

FANNY. Oh, there's a deal of fluke about these things. You see, I had the advantage -

DR. FREEMANTLE [with watch still in his hand]. I THINK, ladies -

ENGLAND. Come on, girls.

[A general movement.]

FANNY. You must all come again—spend a whole day—some Sunday.

CANADA. Remember me to Vernon.

FANNY. He'll be so sorry to have -

ENGLAND [cutting in]. 'Ope we 'aven't upset you, dear. [She is bustling them all up.]

FANNY. Not at all. [She is kissing the girls.] It's been so good to see you all again.

ENGLAND. 'Urry up, girls, there's dears. [To Fanny] Good-bye, dear. [Kissing her.] We DO miss yer.

FANNY. I'm glad you do.

ENGLAND. Oh, it ain't the same show. [The others are crowding out of the door. She and Fanny are quite apart.] No chance of your coming back to it, I suppose? [A moment.] Well, there, you never know, do yer? Good-bye, dear. [Kisses her again.]

FANNY. Good-bye! [She stands watching them out. Bennet goes down with them. Ernest is busy collecting debris. Jane and Honoria stand one each side of the table, rigid, with set faces. After a moment Fanny goes to the open window. The voices of the girls below, crowding into the van, come up into the room. She calls down to them.] Good-bye. You've plenty of time. What? Yes, of course. [Laughs.] All right. Good-bye. [She turns, comes slowly back. She looks at Jane and Honoria, where they stand rigid. Honoria makes a movement with her shoulders—takes a step towards the door.] Honoria! [Honoria stops—slowly turns.] You can take away these glasses. Jane will help you.

[Bennet has reappeared.]

HONORIA. It's not my place -

FANNY. Your place is to obey my orders.

BENNET [his coolness seems to have deserted him. His voice is trembling]. Obey her ladyship's orders, both of you. Leave the rest to me. [Honoria and Jane busy themselves, with Ernest setting the room to rights.] May I speak with your ladyship?

FANNY. Certainly.

BENNET. Alone, I mean.

FANNY. I see no need.

BENNET [her firmness takes him aback. He expected to find her defiance disappear with the cause of it. But pig-headed, as all Bennets, her opposition only drives him on]. Your ladyship is not forgetting the alternative?

[The Misses Wetherell have been watching the argument much as the babes in the wood might have watched the discussion between the two robbers.]

THE ELDER MISS WETHERELL [in terror]. Bennet! you're not going to give notice!

BENNET. What my duty may be, I shall be able to decide after I have spoken with her ladyship—alone.

THE YOUNGER MISS WETHERELL. Dear! You will see him?

FANNY. I am sorry. I have not the time.

THE YOUNGER MISS WETHERELL. No. Of course. [Appealing to Bennet for mercy] Her ladyship is tired. To-morrow -

FANNY [interrupting]. Neither to-morrow—nor any other day. [Vernon enters, followed by Newte. She advances to meet them.] You've just missed some old friends of yours. [She shakes hands with Newte.]

VERNON. So it seems. We were hoping to have been in time. [To Newte] The mare came along pretty slick, didn't she?

BENNET [he has remained with his look fixed all the time on Fanny]. May I speak with your lordship a moment—in private?

VERNON. Now?

BENNET. It is a matter that needs to be settled now. [It is the tone of respectful authority he has always used towards the lad.]

VERNON. Well, if it's as pressing as all that I suppose you must. [He makes a movement towards the door. To Newte] Shan't be long.

FANNY. One moment. [Vernon stops.] I may be able to render the interview needless. Who is mistress of this house?

VERNON. Who is mistress?

FANNY. Who is mistress of your house?

VERNON. Why, you are, of course.

FANNY. Thank you. [She turns to Bennet] Please tell Mrs. Bennet I want her.

BENNET. I think if your lordship -

FANNY. At once. [She is looking at him. He struggles—looks at Vernon. But Vernon is evidently inclined to support Fanny. Bennet goes out. She crosses and seats herself at the desk. She takes from a drawer some neatly folded papers. She busies herself with figures.]

VERNON [he crosses to his Aunts]. Whatever's the matter?

THE ELDER MISS WETHERELL. She is excited. She has had a very trying time.

THE YOUNGER MISS WETHERELL. Bennet didn't like the idea of her receiving them.

NEWTE. It was that minx Judy's doing. They'll have the rough side of my tongue when I get back—all of them.

VERNON. What does she want with Mrs. Bennet?

THE ELDER MISS WETHERELL. I can't think.

[The atmosphere is somewhat that of a sheepfold before a thunderstorm. The Misses Wetherell are still clinging to one another. Vernon and Dr. Freemantle are both watching Fanny. Jane, Honoria, and Ernest are still busy about the room.

Suddenly, to Newte—who is standing apart—the whole thing comes with a rush. But it is too late for him to interfere.

Mrs. Bennet, followed by Bennet, are entering the room. He shrugs his shoulders and turns away.]

MRS. BENNET. Your ladyship sent for me?

FANNY. Yes. [She half turns—holds out a paper.] This wages sheet is quite correct, I take it? It is your own.

MRS. BENNET [she takes it]. Quite correct.

FANNY [she tears out a cheque she has written—hands it to Mrs. Bennet]. You will find there two months' wages for the entire family. I have made it out in a lump sum payable to your husband. The other month is in lieu of notice. [A silence. The thing strikes them all dumb. She puts the cheque-book back and closes the drawer. She rises.] I'm sorry. There's been a misunderstanding. It's time that it ended. It has been my own fault. [To Vernon] I deceived you about my family -

NEWTE. If there's been any deceit -

FANNY. My scene, please, George. [Newte, knowing her, returns to silence.] I have no relations outside this country that I know of. My uncle is Martin Bennet, your butler. Mrs. Bennet is my aunt. I'm not ashamed of them. If they'd had as much respect for me as I have for them, this trouble would not have arisen. We don't get on together, that's all. And this seems to me the only way out. As I said before, I'm sorry.

VERNON [recovering speech]. But why did you—?

FANNY [her control gives way. She breaks out]. Oh, because I've been a fool. It's the explanation of most people's muddles, I expect, if they only knew it. Don't talk to me, anybody. I've got nothing more to say. [To Bennet] I'm sorry. You wouldn't give me a chance. I'd have met you half way. [To Mrs. Bennet] I'm sorry. Don't be too hard on me. It won't mean much trouble to you. Good servants don't go begging. You can depend upon me for a character. [To Jane] You'll do much better for yourselves elsewhere. [To Honoria] Don't let that pretty face of yours ever get you into trouble. [To Ernest] Good-bye, Ernest. We were always pals, weren't we? Good-bye. [She kisses him. It has all been the work of a moment. She comes down again.] Don't think me rude, but I'd like to be alone. We can talk calmly about it all to-morrow morning. [To the Misses Wetherell] I'm so awfully sorry. I wish I could have seen any other way out. [The tears are streaming from her eyes. To Vernon] Take them all away, won't you, dear? We'll talk about it all to-morrow. I'll feel gooder. [She kisses him. To Dr. Freemantle] Take them all away. Tell him it wasn't all my fault. [To Newte] You'll have to stop the night. There are no more trains. I'll see you in the morning. Good night.

[Bennet has collected his troop. Leads them away. Dr. Freemantle, kindly and helpful, takes off Vernon and the two ladies.]

NEWTE [he grips her hand, and speaks in his short, growling way]. Good night, old girl. [He follows the others out.]

FANNY [crosses towards the windows. Her chief business is dabbing her eyes. The door closes with a click. She turns. She puts her handkerchief away. She looks at the portrait of Constance, first Lady Bantock]. I believe it's what you've been telling me to do, all the time.

[CURTAIN]

ACT IV

SCENE

The same. The blinds are down. Ashes fill the grate.

Time.—Early the next morning.

The door opens softly. Newte steals in. He fumbles his way across to the windows, draws the blinds. The morning sun streams in. He listens—no one seems to be stirring. He goes out, returns immediately with a butler's tray, containing all things necessary for a breakfast and the lighting of a fire. He places the tray on table, throws his coat over a chair, and is on his knees busy lighting the fire, when enter the Misses Wetherell, clad in dressing-gowns and caps: yet still they continue to look sweet. They also creep in, hand in hand. The crouching Newte is hidden by a hanging fire- screen. They creep forward till the coat hanging over the chair catches their eye. They are staring at it as Robinson Crusoe might at the footprint, when Newte rises suddenly and turns. The Misses Wetherell give a suppressed scream, and are preparing for flight.

NEWTE [he stays them]. No call to run away, ladies. When a man's travelled—as I have—across America, in a sleeping-car, with a comic-opera troop, there's not much left for him to know. You want your breakfast! [He wheedles them to the table.] We'll be able to talk cosily—before anybody else comes.

[They yield themselves. He has a way with him.]

THE ELDER MISS WETHERELL. We haven't slept all night.

[Newte answers with a sympathetic gesture. He is busy getting ready the breakfast.]

THE YOUNGER MISS WETHERELL. There's something we want to tell dear Vernon—before he says anything to Fanny.

THE ELDER MISS WETHERELL. It's something very important.

NEWTE. We'll have a cup of tea first—to steady our nerves.

THE YOUNGER MISS WETHERELL. It's so important that we should tell him before he sees Fanny.

NEWTE. We'll see to it. [He makes the tea.] I fancy they're both asleep at present.

THE ELDER MISS WETHERELL. Poor boy!

THE YOUNGER MISS WETHERELL. If she only hadn't -

[Dr. Freemantle has entered.]

DR. FREEMANTLE. I thought I heard somebody stirring -

NEWTE. Hush! [He indicates doors, the one leading to her ladyship's apartments, the other to his lordship's.]

THE YOUNGER MISS WETHERELL [turning and greeting him]. It was so kind of you not to leave us last night.

THE ELDER MISS WETHERELL. We were so upset.

[Dr. Freemantle pats their hands.]

THE YOUNGER MISS WETHERELL. We hope you slept all right.

DR. FREEMANTLE. Excellently. Shall be glad of a shave, that's all. [Laughs. Both he and Newte suggest the want of one.]

NEWTE [who has been officiating]. Help yourself to milk and sugar.

DR. FREEMANTLE [who has seated himself]. Have the Bennets gone?

NEWTE. Well, they had their notice all right.

THE YOUNGER MISS WETHERELL [they have begun to cry]. It has been so wrong and foolish of us. We have never learnt to do anything for ourselves.

THE ELDER MISS WETHERELL. We don't even know where our things are.

DR. FREEMANTLE. They can't all have gone—the whole twenty-three of them, at a couple of hours' notice. [To Newte] Haven't seen any of them, have you?

NEWTE. No sign of any of them downstairs.

DR. FREEMANTLE. Oh, they must be still here. Not up, I suppose. It isn't seven o'clock yet.

THE YOUNGER MISS WETHERELL. But they have all been discharged. We can't ask them to do anything.

THE ELDER MISS WETHERELL [to her sister]. And the Grimstones are coming to lunch with the new curate. Vernon asked them on Sunday.

THE YOUNGER MISS WETHERELL. Perhaps there's something cold.

THE ELDER MISS WETHERELL. Vernon so dislikes a cold lunch.

DR. FREEMANTLE [to Newte]. Were you able to get hold of Vernon last night?

NEWTE. Waited up till he came in about two o'clock. Merely answered that he wasn't in a talkative mood— brushed past me and locked himself in.

DR. FREEMANTLE. He wouldn't say anything to me either. Rather a bad sign when he won't talk.

NEWTE. What's he likely to do?

DR. FREEMANTLE. Don't know. Of course it will be all over the county.

THE YOUNGER MISS WETHERELL. And dear Vernon is so sensitive.

DR. FREEMANTLE. It had to come—the misfortune IS -

NEWTE. The misfortune IS that people won't keep to their own line of business. Why did he want to come fooling around her? She was doing well for herself. She could have married a man who would have thought more of her than all the damn fools in the county put together. Why couldn't he have left her alone?

DR. FREEMANTLE [he is sitting at the head of the table, between Newte on his right and the Misses Wetherell on his left. He lays his hand on Newte's sleeve—with a smile]. I'm sure you can forgive a man—with eyes and ears in his head—for having fallen in love with her.

NEWTE. Then why doesn't he stand by her? What if her uncle is a butler? If he wasn't a fool, he'd be thanking his stars that 'twas anything half as respectable.

DR. FREEMANTLE. I'm not defending him—we're not sure yet that he needs any defence. He has married a clever, charming girl of—as you say—a better family than he'd any right to expect. The misfortune is, that—by a curious bit of ill-luck—it happens to be his own butler.

NEWTE. If she takes my advice, she'll return to the stage. No sense stopping where you're not wanted.

THE YOUNGER MISS WETHERELL. But how can she?

THE ELDER MISS WETHERELL. You see, they're married!

DR. FREEMANTLE [to change the subject]. You'll take an egg?

[Newte has been boiling some. He has just served them.]

THE ELDER MISS WETHERELL [rejecting it]. Thank you.

THE YOUNGER MISS WETHERELL. We're not feeling hungry.

THE ELDER MISS WETHERELL. He was so fond of her.

THE YOUNGER MISS WETHERELL. She was so pretty.

THE ELDER MISS WETHERELL. And so thoughtful.

THE YOUNGER MISS WETHERELL. One would never have known she was an actress.

THE ELDER MISS WETHERELL. If only she hadn't -

[Bennet has entered. Newte is at fireplace. The old ladies have their backs to the door. Dr. Freemantle, who is pouring out tea, is the first to see him. He puts down the teapot, staring. The old ladies look round. A silence. Newte turns. Bennet is again the perfect butler. Yesterday would seem to have been wiped out of his memory.]

BENNET. Good morning, Miss Wetherell. Good morning, Miss Edith. [To the two men] Good morning. I was not aware that breakfast was required to be any earlier than usual, or I should have had it ready.

THE YOUNGER MISS WETHERELL. We are sure you would, Bennet. But you see, under the circumstances, we—we hardly liked to trouble you.

BENNET [he goes about the room, putting things to rights. He has rung the bell. Some dead flowers he packs on to Newte's tray, the water he pours into Newte's slop-basin]. My duty, Miss Edith, I have never felt to be a trouble to me.

THE ELDER MISS WETHERELL. We know, Bennet. You have always been so conscientious. But, of course, after what's happened—[They are on the verge of tears again.]

BENNET [he is piling up the breakfast things]. Keziah requested me to apologise to you for not having heard your bell this morning. She will be ready to wait upon you in a very few minutes. [To the Doctor] You will find shaving materials, doctor, on your dressing- table.

DR. FREEMANTLE. Oh, thank you.

[Ernest has entered, with some wood; he is going towards the fire.]

BENNET [to Ernest]. Leave the fire for the present. Take away this tray. [Ernest takes up the tray, and goes out. Bennet speaks over the heads of the Misses Wetherell to Newte] Breakfast will be ready in the morning-room, in a quarter of an hour.

NEWTE [at first puzzled, then indignant, now breaks out]. What's the little game on here—eh? Yesterday afternoon you were given the sack—by your mistress, Lady Bantock, with a month's wages in lieu of notice— not an hour before you deserved it. What do you mean, going on like this, as if nothing had happened? Is Lady Bantock to be ignored in this house as if she didn't exist—or is she not? [He brings his fist down on the table. He has been shouting rather than speaking.] I want this thing settled!

BENNET. Your bath, Mr. Newte, is quite ready.

NEWTE [as soon as he can recover speech]. Never you mind my bath, I want -

[Vernon has entered. He is pale, heavy-eyed, short in his manner, listless.]

VERNON. Good morning—everybody. Can I have some breakfast, Bennet?

BENNET. In about ten minutes; I will bring it up here. [He collects the kettle from the fire as he passes, and goes out.]

VERNON. Thank you. [He responds mechanically to the kisses of his two aunts, who have risen and come to him.]

NEWTE. Can I have a word with you?

VERNON. A little later on, if you don't mind, Mr. Newte. [He passes him.]

NEWTE [he is about to speak, changes his mind]. All right, go your own way. [Goes out.]

DR. FREEMANTLE. "Remember", says Marcus Aurelius -

VERNON. Yes—good old sort, Marcus Aurelius. [He drops listlessly into a chair.]

[Dr. Freemantle smiles resignedly, looks at the Misses Wetherell, shrugs his shoulders, and goes out, closing the door after him.

The Misses Wetherell whisper together—look round cautiously, steal up behind him, encouraging one another.]

THE ELDER MISS WETHERELL. She's so young.

THE YOUNGER MISS WETHERELL. And so adaptable.

VERNON [he is sitting, bowed down, with his face in his hands]. Ah, it was the deception.

THE YOUNGER MISS WETHERELL [she puts her old thin hand on his shoulder]. What would you have done, dear, if she had told you—at first?

VERNON [he takes her hand in his—answers a little brokenly]. I don't know.

THE ELDER MISS WETHERELL. There's something we wanted to tell you. [He looks at her. They look across at each other.] The first Lady Bantock, your great-grandmamma -

THE YOUNGER MISS WETHERELL. She danced with George III.

THE ELDER MISS WETHERELL. She was a butcher's daughter.

THE YOUNGER MISS WETHERELL. He was quite a little butcher.

THE ELDER MISS WETHERELL. Of course, as a rule, dear, we never mention it.

THE YOUNGER MISS WETHERELL. We felt you ought to know. [They take each other's hands; on tip-toe they steal out. They close the door softly behind them.]

[Vernon rises. He looks at the portrait—draws nearer to it. With his hands in his pockets, stops dead in front of it, and contemplates it in silence. The door of the dressing-room opens. Fanny enters. She is dressed for going out. She stands for a moment, the door in her hand. Vernon turns. She closes the door and comes forward.]

VERNON. Good morning.

FANNY. Good morning. George stayed the night, didn't he?

VERNON. Yes. He's downstairs now.

FANNY. He won't be going for a little while?

VERNON. Can't till the ten o'clock train. Have you had breakfast?

FANNY. I—I've had something to eat. I'm sorry for what I did last night—although they did deserve it. [Laughs.] I suppose it's a matter than can easily be put right again.

VERNON. You have no objection to their staying?

FANNY. Why should I?

VERNON. What do you mean?

FANNY. There's only one hope of righting a mistake. And that is going back to the point from where one went wrong—and that was our marriage.

[A moment.]

VERNON. We haven't given it a very long trial.

FANNY [with an odd smile]. It went to pieces at the first. I was in trouble all last night; you must have known it. You left me alone.

VERNON. Jane told me you had locked yourself in.

FANNY. You never tried the door for yourself, dear. [She pretends to rearrange something on the mantelpiece—

any excuse to turn away her face for a moment. She turns to him again, smiling.] It was a mistake, the whole thing. You were partly to blame. You were such a nice boy. I "fancied" you—to use George's words. [She laughs.] And when a woman wants a thing, she is apt to be a bit unscrupulous about how she gets it. [She moves about the room, touching the flowers, rearranging a cushion, a vase.] I didn't invent the bishop; that was George's embroidery. [Another laugh.] But, of course, I ought to have told you everything myself. I ought not to have wanted a man to whom it would have made one atom of difference whether my cousins were scullery-maids or not. Somehow, I felt that to you it might. [Vernon winces.] It's natural enough. You have a big position to maintain. I didn't know you were a lord—that was your doing. George did find it out, but he never told me; least of all, that you were Lord Bantock—or you may be pretty sure I should have come out with the truth, if only for my own sake. It hasn't been any joke for me, coming back here.

VERNON. Yes. I can see they've been making things pretty hard for you.

FANNY. Oh, they thought they were doing their duty. [He is seated. She comes up behind him, puts her hands on his shoulders.] I want you to take them all back again. I want to feel I have made as little commotion in your life as possible. It was just a little mistake. And everybody will say how fortunate it was that she took herself off so soon with that—[She was about to say "that theatrical

Johnny," thinking of Newte. She checks herself.] And you will marry somebody belonging to your own class. And those are the only sensible marriages there are.

VERNON. Have you done talking?

FANNY. Yes! Yes, I think that's all.

VERNON. Then perhaps you'll let me get in a word. You think me a snob? [Fanny makes a movement.] As a matter of fact, I am.

FANNY. No, that's not fair. You wouldn't have married a girl off the music-hall stage.

VERNON. Niece of a bishop, cousin to a judge. Whether I believed it or not, doesn't matter. The sham that isn't likely to be found out is as good as the truth, to a snob. If he had told me your uncle was a butler, I should have hesitated. That's where the mistake began. We'll go back to that. Won't you sit down? [Fanny sits.] I want you to stop. There'll be no mistake this time. I'm asking my butler's niece to do me the honour to be my wife.

FANNY. That's kind of you.

VERNON. Oh, I'm not thinking of you. I'm thinking of myself. I want you. I fell in love with you because you were pretty and charming. There's something else a man wants in his wife besides that. I've found it. [He jumps up, goes over to her, brushing aside things in his way.] I'm not claiming it as a right; you can go if you like. You can earn your own living, I know. But you shan't have anybody else. You'll be Lady Bantock and nobody else— as long as I live. [He has grown quite savage.]

FANNY [she bites her lip to keep back the smile that wants to come]. That cuts both ways, you know.

VERNON. I don't want anybody else.

FANNY [she stretches out her hand and lays it on his]. Won't it be too hard for you? You'll have to tell them all—your friends— everybody.

VERNON. They've got to be told in any case. If you are here, for them to see, they'll be able to understand— those that have got any sense.

[Bennet comes in with breakfast, for two, on a tray. He places it on a table.]

FANNY [she has risen, she goes over to him]. Good morning, uncle. [She puts up her face. He stares, but she persists. Bennet kisses her.] Lord Bantock—[she looks at Vernon]—has a request to make to you. He wishes me to remain here as his wife. I am willing to do so, provided you give your consent.

VERNON. Quite right, Bennet. I ought to have asked for it before. I apologise. Will you give your consent to my marriage with your niece?

FANNY. One minute. You understand what it means? From the moment you give it—if you do give it—I shall be Lady Bantock, your mistress.

BENNET. My dear Fanny! My dear Vernon! I speak, for the first and last time, as your uncle. I am an old-fashioned person, and my ideas, I have been told, are those of my class. But observation has impressed it upon me that success in any scheme depends upon each person being fit for their place. Yesterday, in the interests of you both, I should have refused my consent. To-day, I give it with pleasure, feeling sure I am handing over to Lord Bantock a wife in every way fit for her position. [Kissing her, he gives her to Vernon, who grips his hand. He returns to the table.] Breakfast, your ladyship, is quite ready.

[They take their places at the table. Fanny takes off her hat, Bennet takes off the covers.]

[CURTAIN]

www.ingramcontent.com/pod-product-compliance
Lightning Source LLC
Chambersburg PA
CBHW020205090426
42734CB00008B/953